Z'Art of Gourmet Seduction

A CULINARY EXPRESSION OF LOVE

FOR <u>MEN</u> ONLY

by Master Chef

Jacques Prudhomme

CHAMBERS PUBLISHING GROUP

CLEVELAND, OH

1998

Published in the Western Hemisphere by

Underwood Books Imprint of
Chambers Publishing Group, Inc.
Cleveland, Ohio

Printed in United States of America

Cover and Book Design:
Abram Ross, Inc.
www.abramross.com

Editorial Assistance:
Rena Lacey

10987654321

ISBN No. 1-892509-22-9

*Dedicated to the
Lost Art of Romance*

Table of Contents

Contents

FORWARD

*M*y Friends,

Do not expect *Z'Art of Gourmet Seduction, A Culinary Expression of Love* to be a cookbook like any other one. It is definitely unique.

First, from my heart I say: Congratulations! With this book, you are about to embark on what could be the most romantic episodes of your life—filled with success, pleasure, and fun.

To succeed in these romantic episodes, you must have an open mind. So, just make yourself comfortable, sip a glass of wine, and get involved. Read the whole book first. You will see how powerful and easy it is to use *Z'Art of Gourmet Seduction.* Then go back and experiment with one, or a selection of several menus, for yourself first.

It works for me. Should it work for you? But of course! *Z'Art of Gourmet Seduction* is designed for men but can be used by everyone...men and women. Laugh as you read about my adventures; experience gourmet cooking as you try my recipes; and follow my gourmet seduction advice. You will definitely begin to enjoy life as I do.

Everyone has to eat, right? But how many people know how to entertain successfully?

First, establish your goal. Let's say you are a bachelor with a strong desire to develop a closer friendship with a certain special lady. What do you do? Take her to a fancy restaurant and try to be debonair and charming to her in front of 50 to 200 people? Wrong. Even a rose loses its fragrance around too many obstructing noses.

Take her to your castle, in complete privacy. It will be you, her, the rose, the wine, the soft music...and the meal. And to

display your culinary creation, be sure to remember the candles and the well-set table. I promise that if you follow all my instructions, you will be *z'conqueror* in whatever endeavor you have planned.

Or, say you have an opposite situation in mind—a relationship you really want to discontinue. You would not want to break the news to her in a public place, with tears and sniffles, and maybe spaghetti in your lap. Why not seduce your mate into an everlasting friendship by using *Z'Art of Gourmet Seduction*, along with my philosophy and yours? Could it work? But of course!

You will find, as I have, that *Z'Art of Gourmet Seduction* can be used in many different experiences and situations that you will face in life. If you have the right attitude, entertaining is fun, easy, and very rewarding.

Gentlemen have often asked me, "Jacques, how do you do it? You are always surrounded by beautiful ladies. How do you manage it?"

My response is, "I use *z'art* of gourmet seduction." One of my greatest conquests of the heart a few years ago, was my little bunny. You know, the lovely bunny from the Playboy Club. These gorgeous young ladies are not so easy to catch as you may think, even if you are a good hunter. The Los Angeles Playboy Club was one of my favorite places to go. It had great atmosphere, excellent cuisine, and above all, the best Playboy Bunnies in the world. I must say that Mr. Hefner has excellent taste.

Anyway, the most beautiful bunny at the Club caught my eye and I decided I wanted to get to know her better. This was not easy because Club rules forbid the bunnies to date the customers. She told me this right away, but I was not so easily dissuaded. After a few friendly conversations, she told me that Sunday was her day off and that she went to the beach in Malibu every Sunday. I said nothing more about it at that time. But, the next Sunday, I went to the beach they call Muscle Beach, where all the body builders go. Talk about competition! But I

was not discouraged (I used to pump a little iron myself and was still in good condition). Finally I saw her, surrounded by four or five Greek gods. What a beauty she was. The closer I got, the bigger my chest got. She spotted me, said hi, and introduced me to the gods. I stayed around for several hours, waiting for the right moment to make my move. I finally got the chance to ask her if she'd ever had a gourmet seduction.

"Not really," she said. "I am only twenty-two."

I quickly replied, "You mean to tell me that no man has ever romanced you with a magnificent gourmet dinner with all the frills? No roses, no champagne, etc.?"

"No," she said. "Things like that only happen in the movies."

"Oh, you really think so?" I said. "Well, it's 2:00 p.m. now. Be at my place at 7:00 p.m., and I promise you my very best gourmet seduction."

"You got it," she replied. With a slight giggle, she asked what would be on the menu, "pizza?"

"Trust me," I said. "If you think for a moment that I would insult you or trick you, forget it, Cinderella. I am the best."

"Sorry," she said, "I will be there at seven sharp."

And she was. Believe me, it was a delightfully new adventure for *z'beautiful* little bunny. And I must tell you, it was the beginning of a delicious relationship. My friends, it worked for me, and it will work for you.

Jacques Prudhomme

INTRODUCTION

$\mathcal{T}$his book is about Romancing. *Z'Art of Gourmet Seduction, A Culinary Expression of Love for Men Only* tells, step-by-step, how to create charm and allure in the kitchen and dining room and how to use gourmet seduction to win over someone special. Though the title says For Men Only, these menus and recipes can be used to express love to any special someone—be it a date, a spouse, a friend or family member, or a business acquaintance. When you desire to appeal to the special tastes of someone important, for any important reason, reach for *Z'Art of Gourmet Seduction.*

I believe you will find both the recipes and the *mis en scene* with me, enlightening, as I share with you how to shop for food, prepare it, serve it, and use it as a tool for achieving any purpose. Romancing with food, in the proper way, is fun and exciting. And is it good? But of course!

In this book, you will see how good life can be. Because of my gourmet seduction techniques, I have enjoyed a life filled with romantic episodes. Read my stories and laugh, give my menus and recipes a try, and experience *z'romance* for yourself!

A SPECIAL MESSAGE FROM JACQUES

In order to establish the proper ambiance in my teaching or working relationship with you, think of me as a ghost (like in the movies). Only YOU can see or hear me. This method should prove to be more fun and relaxing. But remember not to answer me, otherwise your dinner partner may think you just escaped from the coo-coo's nest. You could end up having your delicious gourmet seduction with the ghost—me.

Since this book is sold internationally, I have included MSG (monosodium glutamate) in some of the recipes. Personally, I do not use it. There are too many unfavorable reports surround-

ing it. As you will notice, menus are of an international flavor, so you may add or substitute certain herbs or spices, such as Cajun seasonings. Use fresh herbs whenever you can, when available. You can easily grow your own herbs on a porch or in a kitchen window.

You may notice that microwaves are not suggested here. I am not against using them, however, as long as it is for cooking vegetables or reheating previously prepared foods. I just don't like cooking meats, poultry, or fish in the microwave. Most chefs feel the same way—there are no short cuts for quality prepared foods. I'll admit, it is a wonderful invention for quick meals. Since we are living in such fast times and are constantly on the go, we must improvise as life rushes by.

While my book is 'for men only,' it can be used by women too. The menus included are suggested only as a guide—you may select a similar menu to suit your occasion, be it for business, friendship, or fun.

In our changing times, I have noticed that many more men are entertaining and cooking, so I designed the cookbook to help them by giving different examples of occasion menus. Also included is my special diet which can help in keeping your weight under control. I spent many years developing this diet while I was a chef in the Arctic Circle. Since food was the main highlight of the day there, many people got out of shape, so this diet was very useful.

SETTING THE STAGE FOR A GOURMET SEDUCTION

Now you are ready. I usually handwrite the entire menu creation on parchment paper, then roll it up and tie it with a pink ribbon. For instance, I would write something like this:

Z'ART OF GOURMET SEDUCTION

Created Especially for "<u>Her Name Here</u>"

ROMANCE. . . A POWERFUL WORD FOR ALL SEASONS

FOR PEOPLE OF ALL NATIONS

ROMANCE HAS SURVIVED THE SANDS OF TIME

I SEE IT LOOKING IN YOUR EYES

AS TIME GOES BY, REMEMBER ME

ROMANCING YOU IN MY SPECIAL WAY

*** **THE MENU** ***

Bon Appetit,

Your Name Here

Now, my friend, you are ready for the majestic entrance of Cinderella. The one and only from your fantasyland.

Remember, I am there in my ghostly presence, watching and guiding you every step of the way. Here is my sample narration:

As Cinderella rings the doorbell, I see the prince dressed in black slacks and a long-sleeved peach-colored shirt with a relaxed collar. Opening the door of his humble castle, he kisses Cinderella's delicate hand. As she enters, she comments on how

warm and inviting his castle is. He quickly replies, "I am really happy that you feel comfortable, because my castle is your castle." She glances toward the fireplace and admires the glow. This gives the prince a chance to admire his princess—all of her five-foot-four-inch celestial body adorned with the most beautiful sky blue eyes. As she turns to look at the prince, she gives a disarming smile saying how lucky she is to be treated like royalty.

The prince immediately displays his charisma by saying, "Your delightful presence here is totally responsible for the warm hospitality of my castle."

"Thank you," she replies as she sits down on the couch facing the fire.

The prince asks, "Will champagne be to your taste before dinner?"

"That would be delightful," she says.

As I watch the prince enjoying conversation for thirty minutes or so, I feel like he has completely forgotten about dinner. But no, he gets up and escorts Cinderella to the dining room. Pulling her chair out and seating her properly, he lights the candles and puts on the dinner music. Telling Cinderella he will be right back, he walks into the kitchen, turning on the microwave to heat the bisque and the oven for the bread (that is already in). He then picks up a dinner plate covered with a linen napkin and puts a single rose and the wrapped parchment on top. The prince walks back into the dining room, and with a gentle smile on his radiant face, bends slightly down to his princess and says, "This gourmet creation is dedicated to the honor of your being here in my humble castle, and since roses are the flower of romance and an expression of love, I believe they should always be in your presence."

Whoa! He is getting good; this is going to be interesting. While Cinderella is reading her souvenir poem and menu creation and gazing at the rose in front of her, I can feel how much she appreciates the prince's kindness. He walks back in from the

kitchen with a basket of warm bread and butter, saying he will be right back with the bisque. I notice the exchange of warm feelings as they enjoy their bisque. As the prince stands and picks up the empty bowls, he accepts the princess' compliments with great modesty. He returns with the salad and quickly plays another dinner music CD. As casual conversation carries on, he offers her some bread and butter, which she declines. The prince excuses himself once more and says it will only take ten to fifteen minutes to prepare the entree. The princess asks to help, but the prince says, "It is your turn to be pampered, and I cannot allow you to spoil that honor for me." He tells her she is free to examine his record collection while he continues dinner. "Very well," she replies.

I could swear, as I watch the prince in the kitchen, that he is a professional chef. His timing and coordination is perfect. He has the vegetable over the rice in the microwave heating up as he is cooking the veal. Within fifteen minutes, he has artistically arranged the food in the best presentation and cleaned up in the kitchen. I am very proud of my prince as he presents his delicious dinner to his princess. You should see the look on her angelic face.

"This is beautiful!" she says. "I'm sure it will be as delicious as it looks. Are you really a gourmet chef?"

He says, "I really hoped you would be pleased; however, I am not a gourmet chef. I just have a very good teacher. Besides," he continues, "you have inspired me. Your beauty makes me feel artistic." Boy, this kid is smooth. There is no doubt he will conquer.

I can tell that the prince is in seventh heaven by the look of contentment on his face. I wish I could be in his shoes, instead of walking around with a glass shoe in my pocket, looking for my own Cinderella. I have never heard so many compliments in my life. At one point, I really get worried that all this attention will go to the prince's head and blow the whole evening. He keeps his cool, saying things like, "It is okay for a man to

prepare a lovely romantic dinner for a loved one. Why should the woman do all the cooking and romance? Besides, it is an expression of love." He is good, very good.

Dessert emerges from the kitchen—flaming! A fantastic special effect which the prince figured out by himself. He simply took a plain crouton and soaked it in 151 proof rum. It will light up and burn for two or three minutes. The princess asks what kind of fruit is on the dessert. The prince replies, "Since I met you, I have had stars in my mind, so I thought it would be very appropriate for this occasion to slice up some star fruits." He continues, "I really like you, Cinderella. You can make me the most creative and artistic prince on Earth. Sorry, I got carried away. Don't forget, I am in fantasyland." As Cinderella laughs, with a touch of embarrassment, she says, "Who is to say fantasyland does not exist? It would be a better world if everyone had a bit of fantasy in their lives."

WOW! I think I'm going to be sick to my stomach; I am leaving. This sucker bought my cookbook and got his Cinderella on his first gourmet meal. I have been cooking, teaching, and writing books all of my life and am still looking for mine! I can't take it anymore. He certainly doesn't need me.

Well, my friends, do me one favor. Whatever you do, don't ever mistreat your Cinderella. They are not very easy to find and conquer. If you do mistreat yours, I will be right there to take her away from you. Remember, I am the master chef of z'art of gourmet seduction.

The secret to keeping the romance is to not let up for one minute. Look into your spice cabinet—loyalty, honesty, sincerity, and above all, communication, are the ingredients in the recipe for everlasting happiness. When you find it, keep it. Listen to me—I speak from experience. I have been there. Once I forgot to replenish my spice rack and everything went flat. It didn't matter how much I cooked, the taste was not there, so I lost my Cinderella. Maybe I was not the right prince for her.

Who knows? But if you take on the challenge, use fresh herbs and fresh spice. Be creative in your gourmet seductions, try out new recipes. There are no limits to what you can accomplish. The only limitations are in your own mind. Keep thinking that your Cinderella is part of your world and you cannot live without her. It can be very lonely without her in this fast paced world of ours. *Bon Appetit!*

Jacques

MORE IDEAS FOR GOURMET SEDUCTIONS

Here are two more samples of menus to give your romantic heart a jump-start. I created one for a lovely television producer, who was so touched by my romantic creation, she wept. The second was from yet another memorable dinner.

March 18, 1985 For the past twenty years this day has been recorded as the ultimate moment on this planet Earth, when an angelic soul from a far distance of the Universe, entered into the beautiful body of Tami.

Gastronomy of Love

Appetizer
> *Escargots en Chemise*

Salad
> *Of the Athen's Garden*

Entree
> *Fruits of the Seven Seas*

Vegetable
> *Wild Rice-Stuffed Belgian Endive*

Dessert
> *Cupid Layer Cake*

Bon Appetit.
Created with love by
Jacques Prudhomme

An Inspiration for Robin

Appetizer
Goquilles Floridienne

Salad
Gardiniere au Roquefort

Entree
Homard Robin

Vegetables
Riz Sauvage-Haricots Almandine

Dessert
Cygnes au Cacau

Coffee
Café Royal

Bon Appetit.
Created with love by
Jacques Prudhomme

Romancing Heart

*T*he burning flame of love strikes everyone sooner or later. In my life, I've had many attacks.

I especially recall my very first one. I was thirteen years old and still working at the circus, when I came face-to-face with the most beautiful young lady that my eyes had ever before encountered.

First, my little heart began pounding so fast that I broke out in a sweat, you know. So my guardian said to me, "Jacques, this young lady is a guest of the circus. Why don't you show her around?"

"But, of course," I said. Guess what she did? First she said, "He is so cute." Then she grabbed me in her arms, gave me a big hug, and kissed me on the cheek. I almost passed out and could not understand what was happening to me. Never in my life had I experienced something like this. She took my hand, and I gave her a tour of the circus. I was so excited that I would have done anything to impress her—like walking the high wire (it would have been easy; I was already flying), climbing into the lions' cage, riding the elephants, or even swallowing swords and eating fire, you know. However, my romance was a very

short one. She had to leave the next afternoon. But she did not leave empty-handed; she left with my broken heart. I really thought the end of the world was near. Just imagine, a seventeen-year-old beauty walking into my life, hugging me, holding my hand for three hours, telling me that I was very seductive with my big brown eyes, and that lots of girls would be in line for me soon, if I developed charisma and a talent to impress them.

You know, my friends, for many days and lonely nights of very private dreams, I tried to understand the meaning of it all. I came to realize that she was responsible for my development and creation of *Z'Art of Gourmet Seduction*. I became a *chef de cuisine* and then decided I was ready to get my feet wet.

Here's how it went. First, I was at a dance party with a couple of friends. We had just spotted a really attractive young lady, so my two friends asked her for a dance. She turned them down. They were really upset, so I giggled and said to them, "The only tools you have are your feet; you need more than that."

"Oh yeah?" they replied. "If you are so smart, go ahead, it is your turn."

So I went to the bathroom to check my necktie, slick my hair, and do some mental practice. Then I came back to the party and noticed that she was picking up some food from the buffet. So I graciously managed to be next to her and softly whispered in her ear...

"*Mademoiselle*, I don't believe you should eat this. It will endanger your most beautiful complexion. Why not indulge in this...or that...and this would be much better for you," as I pointed out different foods to her.

"Thank you," she replied, with a most rewarding smile. "How do you know all about that?" she asked.

"Well, you know, food is my hobby, and I love to entertain, especially candlelight dinners for two."

"Really," she said, "You mean you can prepare a gourmet dinner all by yourself?"

"But of course," I replied. "I get very creative when I meet someone as beautiful and exciting as you."

"Thank you," she responded. "No gentleman that I know has ever done that for me."

"That will be no longer true, because I feel very strongly that this Saturday night you may bring out of me my very best creation of all. By the way, my name is Jacques Prudhomme. Yours?"

"Suzanne."

So I took her hand and gently kissed it. "The pleasure is all mine," I said. "Should I pick you up at seven or seven-thirty Saturday night?"

"Seven-thirty would be perfect." So we exchanged phone numbers. I told her I would call Thursday for her address. Quickly and graciously, I disappeared. Why? Never give someone the chance to change their mind because you are either talking too much or stepping on their toes while dancing. Keep in mind that you have won the first round. The next round should be undertaken with proper timing, when fascination and gratitude is on your side, you know?

This was my so-anticipated gourmet seduction menu. Remember that I observed the food Suzanne was picking for her plate, so I knew what foods I was going to use.

Romancing Heart

Menu 1

One Rose

Stuffed Mushroom Caps with Capers

Hearts of Palm au Tarragon

Filet Mignon with Sauce Dijon

Almond Rice with Red Bell Pepper

Pears Amaretto

One half bottle white Bordeaux

One half bottle red Beaujolais

Stuffed Mushroom Caps with Capers

Clean and remove stems from **4 large mushroom caps.**
Combine and stuff caps with this mixture:

> **2 tablespoons grated Swiss cheese**
>
> **2 tablespoons drained capers**
>
> **1 tablespoon grated Parmesan cheese**
> **dash of white pepper**

Sprinkle stuffed caps with paprika. Place in baking dish and bake in 375° oven for 20 minutes. Serve with chilled white Bordeaux.

Hearts of Palm au Tarragon

Prepare two chilled salad plates. Place on each plate,

1 large leaf iceburg lettuce.

Then arrange on lettuce:

hearts of palm, cut in quarters

2 large pitted black olives, cut in half

Mix together very well and pour over hearts of palm before serving:

4 tablespoons tarragon vinegar

1 teaspoon sugar

dash of salt and pepper

Filet Mignon with Sauce Dijon

In very hot frying pan, melt **3 tablespoons butter.**

When butter is dark brown, place in pan:
> **2 7-ounce filets of beef, center cut**

Sear for two minutes on each side. Then pour over beef:
> **1 ounce brandy**

Stand back and ignite. Reduce heat to medium and cook steaks on both sides for 2 minutes more for rare, or 3 minutes more for medium. Remove steaks and keep them warm.

To liquid in pan, add:
> **2 ounces Dijon mustard**

Cook 1 minute, stirring constantly. Then add:
> **4 ounces fresh whipping cream**
> **2 tablespoons fresh minced parsley**
> **dash of salt**

Cook until sauce becomes smooth. Pour over steaks. Display your vegetables and serve.

Almond Rice and Red Bell Pepper

Broil **1 large whole red bell pepper.** Peel it. Cut in half lengthwise (remove seeds from inside), and place in baking pan.

In a medium hot frying pan, melt:

2 ounces butter (1/2 stick)

Add and cook until light brown:

2 tablespoons sliced almonds

Then add:

1 cup cooked long-grain white rice

(follow manufacturer's cooking instructions)

dash of salt

Fill peppers with this mixture. Bake in 375° oven for 10 minutes. Serve with entree and red wine.

Pears Amaretto

Peel and core **2 large pears**. Slice lengthwise into 6 pieces each.

Soak for about one hour in:
    4 ounces amaretto

In medium hot frying pan, melt and heat until light brown:
    2 ounces butter (1/2 stick)

Drain pears and sprinkle on both sides with:
    2 tablespoons powdered sugar

Fry the pears 2 minutes on both sides. Add amaretto to pears. Cook 2 minutes more on both sides. Remove pears and place them on a dessert plate in a fan shape. Simmer to reduce the liquid in frying pan, until it is a light syrup. Pour over pears and serve.

RÉSUMÉ

*D*on't be nervous, my friend. I will help you. This is a very easy gourmet seduction. You could be sipping on a glass of wine just for relaxation, but stay away from the amaretto. You need it for cooking.

First, let's check the dining table. Looks as if you've done this before. Everything is perfect—candles, flowers, and a rose, beautiful under-platters (or charger plates), wine glasses for both red and white wines, and a water glass. It's a nice place setting. I suggest steak knives, a dull knife can ruin your steaks. Also, a lady always prefers dimmer light. I remember one time I had a gourmet seduction in a two-room shack with a wood stove and a fuel lantern, you know. But it turned out to be sensational and romantic. Well, enough yakkety-yak. Kitchen, here we come!

Next, let's broil the pepper and clean the mushrooms. Stuff them, but don't cook them now. Take out the meat—it will cook better. Let's do the pears, then the hearts of palm, and then the sauce. Okay now, line up the ingredients needed. Did you chill the white wine? Good, but I would also uncork the red so it can breathe—the bouquet and taste will be at its best. You are ready. I cannot stay here long. You will be super. Just remember, don't rush the lady. When she arrives, just say, "It feels so right for us to have our first gourmet seduction." You may venture to kiss her hand, but only if you feel comfortable doing it, you know?

Offer a glass of champagne or a cocktail. Talk to her in very light conversation with romantic background music, and please take that necktie off!

Look 'in charge,' but be relaxed. Never let the lady know that you are a novice; she will never know the difference. Besides, keep in mind that ladies are always intimidated by your preparation of a gourmet seduction. You are already ahead of the game. So don't screw up, proceed with *z'gourmet* seduction. At the end of the last course, move right away to the living room with either coffee or liqueur, then give the lady a tour of your habitat, while you study her emotions and kind remarks. Remember, don't push. Well, I am sure that you don't need me any more. So break *z'leg*. See you next time. *A Bientot.*

Feelings

eelings are probably the deepest form of expression between two persons. I have experienced all kinds of feelings, you know, in my life—love, depression, hatred, sympathy, sorrow, loneliness, happiness, excitement, and just feeling good about myself.

Feeling not just good, but great, about yourself is very important to success in your everyday fulfillment of life. For you to succeed in *z'art* of gourmet seduction, you must first build your confidence by saying how great you feel about yourself, even if your first gourmet seduction did not work out quite right, or you goofed up your last one. These things do happen sometimes. The worst thing you can do is to give up. You cannot do that, you know.

I had a terrible experience on one of my first gourmet seductions. But I learned from it—I learned not to lose my cool in sticky situations. Listen as I recall to you this failure of mine…

There must have been a full moon that night because everything went wrong. First, the lady arrived forty-five minutes late. I hated that! Instead of giving her the benefit of the doubt, I let my imagination go wild and created a bad 'who cares' atti-

tude. I should have used her late arrival to my advantage. But no way, José; I was too dumb for that.

When she arrived, I said to her in a cool voice, "Darling, I thought you got cold feet." Well, it was cold all right—the dinner, the lady, the whole night. I should have said, "Darling, I hope you're not upset. I ate most of those delicious appetizers. I knew you were coming, but I could not resist the temptation. I ate one every time that I went into the kitchen. Since I ate my portion, you must share yours with me." But *au contraire*, I managed to make things even worse by rushing every course down her throat. That was a big mistake, you know. She got so full, that by 11 p.m., she was so sleepy, she left.

My poor attitude was my worst mistake. Even before I served the main course, I made the remark, "Well, I hope this is not overcooked, and I hope that you like it." Even if it was overcooked, I should have said, "*Voila...*my best creation just for you, my delicious one, and I know you will love it, because I know that you have excellent taste." That is positive, and it would have worked for me, you know. Most ladies take compliments much better than criticisms or bad attitude, and had I not goofed, this lady would have come back for more. Instead, my only souvenir from her was her toothpick that she left in the ashtray. I should have stuck myself in *z'butt* with it. Too bad, because she was an appetizer all by herself, you know.

What did I learn from that disastrous evening? Not to lose my cool and how to turn a bad situation in my favor. If sometime you must scrap either the soup or the appetizers, don't worry—only you know the menu. (Just be sure to throw away the menu on the rolled parchment!)

I remember one time I had to scrap the entree (the main course)! It was definitely overcooked and nothing is worse than overcooked seafood. What did I do? Simple. I served appetizers, salad, a large display of fresh fruits and cheeses with hot French bread. I always keep these on hand for those little emergencies, like when someone just drops in. You can always get by

with this—it works.

Here is the menu I used that night I was left holding *z'toothpick*. If I had been more positive, she probably would even have eaten *z'toothpick*, and our romance would have peaked, you know!

*F*eelings

Menu 2

One Rose

Oysters Babilonne

Sweet and Sour Hearts of Artichoke

Crevettes Campagnarde (Country Style Prawns)

Vegetables en Casserole

Strawberries au Chocolat

White Chablis

Oysters Babilonne

Clean and open **12 small fresh oysters.** Pry loose and reserve bottom shell. Try to save as much nectar as possible.

In cold water soak:

> **marinated grape leaves from 16-ounce jar**

Soak for 1 hour. Change water after 30 minutes.

Cut into 12 small chunks:

> **1/4 pound feta cheese**

Spread leaves. Put one oyster in center of each leaf.

Top each oyster with:

> **a sprinkle of Greek seasoning**
> **dash of tabasco sauce**
> **a piece of the feta cheese**

Wrap the grape leaves around the oysters and put back into shells. Top with **one-half ripe olive.** Bake at 400° for 12 minutes. Serve at once.

Sweet and Sour Hearts of Artichoke

Mix in small saucepan:

    4 ounces distilled white vinegar

    6 ounces sugar (1 cup less 3 tablespoons)

    2 ounces olive oil

    1/8 teaspoon pickling spices

    1/8 teaspoon salt

Bring to a boil. Reduce to medium heat and simmer for 20 minutes. Pass through a sieve or colander.

In deep container place:

    1 8-ounce can plain artichoke hearts, drained

Pour prepared liquid over hearts and chill for 3 hours.

When ready to serve, place on each salad plate:

    a large piece of lettuce

    half the artichoke hearts

    3 tablespoons of the sauce

Crevettes Campagnarde
(Country Style Prawns)

Peel, devein, and dry with a paper towel:
8 jumbo shrimps

Have at hand:
1/2 pound thin-sliced bacon
and a mixture of:
1 tablespoon seafood seasonings
1 tablespoon flour

Roll each shrimp in flour mixture. Shake off excess flour mixture, and wrap with a slice of bacon. Lay shrimps on a baking pan. Bake in 375° oven for 20 minutes.

Decorate with:
6 branches of parsley
wedges from 1 fresh lemon

Serve with vegetables.

NOTE: If you like the bacon crispier, it may be cooked partially (say, one-third done) before you wrap shrimps.

.

Vegetables en Casserole

To prepare white sauce, melt in saucepan over medium heat:

1-1/2 tablespoons butter

Add:

1-1/2 tablespoons flour

Cook 1 minute, stirring constantly. Do not let it change color. Keep stirring while adding:

1/2 cup milk

When sauce is smooth and medium thick, add:

1/4 cup grated Swiss cheese

1 tablespoon Parmesan cheese

dash of each salt, white pepper, and coriander or nutmeg

Set aside. Then wash well:

2 medium carrots, peeled

1 zucchini

2 scallions

6 mushrooms

Slice carrots very thin. Place them in a steamer for 8 minutes. Add zucchini, sliced 1/8-inch thick, and sliced mushrooms. Steam for 7 minutes more. Remove from steamer and place in baking dish. Pour sauce over. Bake at 375° for 10 minutes. Serve.

Strawberries au Chocolat

In a double boiler, melt **8-ounces semi-sweet choco-late** (or melt in microwave, following the instructions on the chocolate's packaging).

Wash and dry **6 large strawberries**, leaving stems on. Holding by the stem, dip each strawberry into the chocolate. Place berries on a plate with a sheet of foil paper to prevent sticking.

Refrigerate until chocolate is firm. Arrange berries on an attractive plate. Serve.

RÉSUMÉ

$\mathcal{I}$ explained, my friend, how you should never lose your cool. But I assure you there is no reason to. I have created this gourmet seduction for you so you can stay in control. It is most unique because everything can be prepared ahead of time.

Not all ladies will be on time. In fact, I waited seven months for one to arrive (I invited her while on one of my adventures in France). She did show up, you know.

Ladies are sometimes 15 to 45 minutes late. So be prepared to keep your cool; otherwise the gourmet seduction could go in reverse.

I have learned that some ladies prefer to keep their first impression intact, so just say, "I am glad you are late. You know, we must have excellent telepathy between us. I was afraid of not being ready on time, but I have just finished my preparation." She definitely will love that. You may not realize, but this is a big point in your favor. Do not say, "No big deal. You just have to stay longer." Bad. That doesn't work.

Since everything can be prepared ahead of time, you really don't need me here tonight. Besides, I have my own gourmet seduction to plan. Just make sure you begin with the artichoke, and finish with strawberries. As for the entree, bake it at the same time you bake the vegetable casserole. Keep your cool. See you soon. *A Bientot*

𝒯issing 𝐿ink

𝒯issing links are when we do things in our life that cause us to look back and ask ourselves, "Why did I do that?" To illustrate, I will recall one of my adventures in gourmet seduction at the North Pole, within the Arctic Circle in Canada.

It all began with a positive attitude that I have developed— "I can do anything that I choose." One day I found myself in the Arctic with the Inuits and very little civilization for five years. I was a chef in charge of providing three meals a day, seven days per week, for a group of approximately thirty Dewline radar operators and workers of all trades—up to 500 workers, depending on where they sent me. I arrived with two years experience in successful gourmet seductions for some beautiful young ladies, along with a promising iron-pumped body. There I was, in the cold, and I mean cold in every way…the climate, the absence opportunities to practice *z'art* of gourmet seduction, the booze, everything. I managed to survive, though, and experienced many unique adventures using my favorite weapon, you know—food. In fact, I managed to keep it alive in different ways and also embarked on many strange adventures by using my favorite weapon, you know—food. It was there that I discovered how powerful a weapon food can be. I kept *z'art* of

gourmet séduction alive by learning how to use it in different ways—like breaking *z'ice* with the natives, or getting special permission for taking trips—I began to understand how to make it work for me.

I created a reputation for myself that allowed me to at least enjoy life in that most unfavorable place on Earth. I must say, however, that I had some unforgettable experiences, like discovering Inuit villages completely unconnected to the civilized world. I learned their culture—fishing, trapping, whaling, and hunting polar bears. I even had a two week self-survival trip, to hunt caribou and reindeer, with my own dog sled! By the way, the only thing I shot was my 35 mm camera. I survived a few plane crashes. I experienced being lost in a snow storm and being chased by a polar bear. (Those suckers can roll downhill a lot faster than I thought!)

Once I was sent to a different radar station with about 75 people to feed. After a couple of weeks there, I learned there was a forbidden Inuit village and trading post across the lake. I had heard from the R.C.M. police that an attractive school teacher from Alberta had just arrived, but that she was not too friendly. I was determined to go, so one night about 9:00 p.m., I walked across the frozen lake and went to the village for a short visit. They were right—she was an exceptional beauty of some 26 years. Unfortunately, the cold must have gotten to her, you know. It was hard to break *z'ice*. I told myself that sooner or later, she would tire of the outpost menu.

Guess what? Two weeks later, she came to my station! We shared food and conversation. As I turned on *z'charm*, she melted a little and accepted my invitation for a gourmet seduction at her shack the next Sunday night. Don't forget, it was forbidden for me to go there, so I had no permissible transportation. Since it was during the endless night dark cycle, no one saw me leaving with a pack full of my "weapons"—the only things missing were *z'rose* and *z'wine*. I thought I was out of practice, but no! The evening was most rewarding, and we planned another hope-

fully closer encounter for the next Sunday

On my way back to the station, I fell between the ice break just on my last jump. It was so cold that my thermal clothing was frozen solid. It was hard to walk, but I didn't get caught, you know! Believe me, it was ironic spending the evening melting *z'ice*, then getting iced myself on my return.

I readied myself for the complete meltdown the next Sunday. But, sadly, it never happened. I received an emergency transfer to the main base on Saturday. Maybe it was just as well; I could very well have gotten iced forever.

All-in-all I never regretted my five years of Arctic isolation. The experience provided me with five years of solitude, to really "find myself," expand my mind, you know. Was I lonely up there? But of course! That is why I kept busy. And if I had not mastered *z'art* of gourmet seduction, I could not have done all that I did. The main reason the station chef allowed me all those forbidden trips and adventures is that I knew *z'art*.

My new goal was to own my own restaurant. Would that be in *z'North Pole*? No, no! First in Mickey Mouse town (Anaheim), California, where there is no snow, and later, in sunny Florida.

If *z'art* of gourmet seduction can work at the North Pole, can it work for you in civilization? But of course!

$\mathcal{M}issing\ \mathcal{L}ink$

Menu 3

One Rose

Alaskan King Crab Legs with Lemon Butter

Mixed Vegetable Salad with Lime Sauce

Poached Salmon Hollandaise

Broiled Tomato and Potato a la Romano

Flaming Baked Alaska

White Zinfandel or Bordeaux Wine

Alaskan King Crab Legs with Lemon Butter

Break legs and claws of **1 pound Alaskan king crab legs**. Take out crabmeat, pat dry, and refrigerate for 30 minutes.

Melt slowly:

> **1/4 pound butter**

Skim butterfat and add:

> **juice of 1 lemon (about 2 tablespoons)**

Heat 2 minutes. Pour into two small dipping dishes. Place in center of plate. Cut **parsley sprigs** and arrange on plates. Arrange the crab meat, cut into 1-inch long pieces, over the parsley. Serve.

Mixed Vegetable Salad with Lime Sauce

Have ready:

> 1/4 cup peanut oil
>
> juice of one lime
>
> 1 tablespoon sugar
>
> 1/8 teaspoon each salt, pepper

In deep, narrow chilled bowl mix:

> 2 egg yolks
>
> 1/8 teaspoon dry mustard

Beat 1 minute with electric beater. Keep beating and add peanut oil a little at a time. When it gets too thick, add a little lime juice, sugar, salt, and pepper. Do this until all ingredients are used. Refrigerate 20 minutes, while preparing vegetables.

Clean, peel, and dice:

> 1 medium tomato
>
> 1 small cucumber
>
> 2 celery stalks
>
> 6 radishes

Wash and break **1 head butter lettuce**. Mix together with other vegetables and chill. Pour salad dressing over chilled vegetables just before serving.

Poached Salmon Hollandaise

Set oven at 375°.

Pour into 3-inch baking pan:

> **6 ounces chablis (wine)**
>
> **4 ounces fish bouillon**
>
> **1/2 teaspoon salt**

Place in oven for 20 minutes. Check and remove small bones from **2 8-ounce salmon fillets**, bone out. Place salmon in pan, bake for about 10 to 12 minutes. Check after 8 minutes to make sure it does not overcook. Remove. Place fillets on plates and keep warm.

In a double boiler mix:

> **4 egg yolks**
>
> **1/8 teaspoon dry mustard**

Beat vigorously with wire whip, then add a portion of:

> **1/4 pound melted butter**
>
> **juice of one lemon**

Continue beating. Remove double boiler from heat. Keep adding butter and lemon juice until all is used. Finish with a dash of **tabasco sauce**.

To prevent sauce from breaking, top boiler pan should be warm, not hot. If sauce starts breaking, quickly add 1 tablespoon cold water and keep beating. For better

prevention, make sauce before poaching salmon. Spoon out sauce evenly over salmon, sprinkle with paprika, decorate with parsley and vegetables and serve.

Broiled Tomato

Cut **1 tomato** in half. Remove bottom core and place in baking pan. Sprinkle with salt, pepper, and bread crumbs. Dot with butter. Bake on top shelf in 450° oven for 15 minutes.

Potato a la Romano

Bake **2 potatoes** in 450° oven for 45 minutes. Cool 10 minutes. Slit potato open and scoop out the meat. Do not pierce the main shell.

Mix potato meat with:

> **1/4 cup grated Romano cheese**
> **1/8 cup fresh whipping cream**
> **dash of white pepper**

Refill potato shells. Dot with butter. Bake on top shelf of oven at 450° for 15 minutes.

Flaming Baked Alaska

Beat **6 egg whites** until firm. Add 6 tablespoons **powdered sugar** and beat 3 minutes. Set aside.

On a sheet pan layered with foil, place:
> **2 individual sponge cakes**
> **(the ones used for strawberry shortcake)**

Divide into 2 servings and place on top of cakes:
> **8 ounces vanilla ice cream**

Spread meringue around entire surface, making sure they are sealed. Freeze for 30 minutes.

Heat oven for broiling. Place pan on bottom shelf of oven. Broil until golden brown. Watch constantly. Remove from oven.

Heat:
> **1 ounce brandy**
> **1 ounce triple sec**

Ignite and stand back. While it is flaming, pour over Alaska and serve.

RÉSUMÉ

$\mathcal{Y}$ou don't have to be in the Arctic Circle to create a cozy, romantic gourmet seduction of your own, you know. This menu brings Alaska to you. Just set up the coffee table for your dinner, light up *z'fireplace*, put *z'pillows* on the floor, kick off *z'shoes*. It is romantic, relaxing, and if you two get a little tipsy, no worry about falling down, you know? Don't think for a minute that ladies don't go for it. You may be surprised.

My intention is for you not to be spending hours in *z'kitchen*—better on *z'floor!* This gourmet creation can be prepared ahead of time except for the salmon. And the vegetables all go in at the same time. I suggest that you bring the dessert to the table, then flame it in front of the lady. But not too close! You could get into big trouble—too hot to handle. . .wigs, slaps, lawsuits!

Keep in mind not to rush *z'dinner.* A slow pace will work better for you, unless the lady just came to fill up on food. Leave room for love. Most likely, though, she came for you, your company, your…gourmet seduction! Well, au revoir—three is a crowd! *A Bientot.*

An Expression of Love

*L*ove is a magic word that has an effect on everyone. Each of us has our own special way of expressing love. My way, you can guess, happens to be the *z'art* of gourmet seduction. For me, there is nothing more rewarding than bringing happiness by doing something for others.

Once I decided to "head for the hills" to spend some time. My connections in food services have always given me the opportunity to go and live anywhere I chose. So I chose the Appalachian Mountains of western North Carolina—Beech Mountain near Boone, more specifically. I became a food and beverage consultant for the area's resort operations including the "Land of Oz" attraction.

It feels so good to be on top of a mountain range and enjoy a breath-taking, panoramic view of three states all at once. It is very good for everyone to have a change of scenery from time-to-time.

I had heard alot about country folks, but let me tell you—life in those hills was so refreshing and peaceful that I spent two restful years there. I have only love and respect for those lucky people—they are so honest and friendly. When I first got there,

they looked at me as a "forner," because for the first couple of months, we didn't understand much of each others' accents.

I was a bachelor at that time, so I decided to put *z'art* of gourmet seduction to work. Truthfully, I had no idea how it would work for me with those Tarheels. After a couple of weeks of developing friendships, I heard that there was on the mountain a beautiful young lady with big blue eyes. Unfortunately, rumors said she was in seclusion because of a broken heart. All the guys there told me, "Don't even try." That was all I needed, a real challenge. So I gave it my best shot.

My gourmet seduction must have been very potent, because it lasted about seven years—seven beautiful and memorable years, I might add. When you make a friend in those hills, the friendship seems to last forever. Even now in my life, I am still surrounded with the same friends I met in the North Carolina High Country. In my heart forever are thousands of cherished memories which will always comfort me.

You are wondering by now, what was the magic gourmet seduction I used on the blue-eyed lady. Here it is:

An Expression of Love

Menu 4

One Rose

Seafood Bisque

Romaine Lettuce with Tarragon Dressing

Roast Duckling St. Jacques

Wild Rice

Artichoke Bottoms au Champignons

Honey Baked Apples

White Chardonnay

Seafood Bisque

Mince very fine and set aside:

> 1/4 pound scallops
>
> 1/4 pound bay shrimp
>
> 1/4 pound crabmeat

To make roux in a 2-quart saucepan, blend together:

> 2 tablespoons butter
>
> 2 tablespoons flour

Cook over medium heat. Add:

> 8 ounces clam juice

Continue stirring. Add:

> 4 ounces chicken bouillon
>
> 1/8 teaspoon seafood seasoning

Cook until smooth. Add:

> 2 egg yolks
>
> 4 ounces fresh whipping cream (lightly beaten)

Cook 3 minutes. Add:

> the minced seafood mixture
>
> 2 tablespoons minced parsley

Simmer on low heat for 10 minutes. If bisque gets too thick, add a little milk. Serve.

Romaine Lettuce with Tarragon Dressing

1 head romaine lettuce, washed and broken into pieces

Put these ingredients into a jar:

> **1/8 cup olive oil**
>
> **1/8 cup tarragon vinegar**
>
> **1 tablespoon sugar**
>
> **1/4 teaspoon each salt and pepper**

Shake very well. Refrigerate for 30 minutes. Pour over lettuce. Mix well and serve.

Roast Duckling St. Jacques

Wash **one 4-pound young duckling** and place on baking pan with rack in bottom.

Pour over duckling:

4 ounces white wine

Peel and section **1 orange**. Insert orange sections between skin of legs and breast by pushing finger between skin and meat (Orange pieces will dissolve fat). Insert orange peel inside duckling.

Sprinkle duckling with:

salt, pepper, and rosemary

Bake at 360° for 90 minutes, basting every 25 minutes with drippings. Take out 2 to 3 tablespoons of drippings. Pour into a saucepan over medium heat.

Mince and sauté in drippings for 3 minutes:

2 medium shallots

Add:

2 tablespoons flour

Cook 2 minutes and add:

8 ounces chicken bouillon

Stir constantly until smooth. Add:

8 ounces fresh blackberries
(reserve a dozen berries for decoration)

Simmer over low heat for 20 minutes. Pass through a sieve and cheese cloth in order to remove all seeds. Put mixture back into saucepan, on low heat.

Add:

3 ounces blackberry brandy

Simmer for 10 minutes. When duckling is cooked, let it stand in a warm place for 15 minutes. Cut in half, remove backbones. Place on plate. Pour approximately 4 tablespoons of sauce over each duckling half. Decorate with rice, artichokes, and place a few of the whole blackberries on top. Serve.

Wild Rice

Wash **4 ounces wild rice** in cold water twice. Let soak for 30 minutes and drain.

Then add:

> **8 ounces water**
>
> **8 ounces chicken bouillon**
>
> **1/4 teaspoon salt**
>
> **1/8 teaspoon pepper**

Bring to a boil. Reduce heat to low, cover tightly, and cook until most of liquid has been absorbed. Rice should be nice and fluffy; with a fork, turn rice over a couple of times. Sometimes you may have to add a little water if grains are completely open. Keep warm and serve.

Artichoke Bottoms au Champignons

Drain, rinse, pat dry, and place in baking pan:

1 can artichoke bottoms

Mix together:

1/2 cup minced mushrooms

1/4 cup grated Swiss cheese

dash each of paprika, salt, and pepper

Stuff artichokes with this mixture. Bake at 375° for 15 minutes. Serve.

Honey Baked Apples

Core with a pointed knife about 2/3 of the way:

2 golden apples

Mix together:

2 ounces raw honey

2 ounces butter (1/2 stick)

juice of one lemon

Fill center of apples with honey mixture. Wrap apples with foil paper, leaving about one-third of the top of the apple exposed. Place on sheet pan. Bake at 350° for 20 minutes. Serve.

RÉSUMÉ

$\mathcal{B}$ack to the hills! I do believe that you should save this gourmet seduction for the hills. It doesn't have to be the Appalachian Mountains; it could be any mountain range.

There is nothing better for an expression of love and a gourmet seduction than a warm and cozy chalet set in a mountain range. The romantic setup is at its best, you know. Even if there is no snow or ski lift, the chalet, the woods, or a lake will give you the feeling of *z'Don Juan* at work.

One thing to keep in mind: Don't even think of bringing your shotgun and hunting for ducks. You'd better pack all needed ingredients—some mountain resorts or retreats may not have them on hand, you know. Play it safe.

By the way, it does not have to be a new lady in mind for that most effective gourmet seduction. It could be your spouse or your permanent lady friend. One thing's for sure, you are guaranteed a complete success even if there are feathers on *z'duck*! Very few ladies can resist your gourmet seduction in a romantic setting like this. The mountain air and the panorama have a special, long-lasting effect on people. Remember, my lady with *z'blue* eyes lasted for seven years. Keep in mind, if you are only looking for a quickie, you may get caught up in your own game. As for romantic atmosphere, except for getting *z'fireplace* fired up, you do not have to worry. It is all built in. So this gourmet seduction is very easy.

First, get started with *z'duck*, then the salad and dressing. Stuff the apples and prepare the vegetables. Take a break. Sip some wine or enjoy a cocktail. Savor *z'aroma* of *z'duck* because each time that you open the oven to baste it, the aroma will fill the room! Toward the last 30 minutes, start on the bisque, then

the sauce for *z'duck*. And don't forget, the artichokes can bake along with the apples.

My friend, I wish I could stay with you. But *z'flat* land has a hold on me at this time. However, I will soon head for the hills for relaxation, and you can bet I will pack a gourmet seduction with me. So enjoy your stay, and drop a postcard if you decide to stay for awhile. See you soon. *A Bientot.*

Lonely at Heart

Loneliness, to me, is probably the most self-inflicted pain. When we start feeling loneliness, we accept it by saying, "I guess this is my destiny." This is baloney, you know.

Each one of us is in complete charge of our own destiny. I have learned that if you like yourself, then you can take charge—and if you do not like what is happening, you can change. It is not as hard as you think. Just feed your subconscious mind with your goals and desires for a change to your dull or unhappy life.

There were times in my life that I did not really enjoy, so I looked into myself and decided to adopt a more positive attitude. Let's face it—we must accept the fact that we are stuck with ourselves for this lifetime. Life can be as exciting as we make it. One secret is self-appreciation—I have found that making yourself miserable is much harder than choosing to be happy. You can shape your life into a more desirable one.

For me, there is no more exciting way of changing my life around than meeting new people, using my charm, engaging in conversation, and planning an invitation for a gourmet seduction, of course! Very few ladies have turned down my invitations, you know. You certainly don't have to be a master chef to

entertain. Just a little practice will do it. Here are a few tips on how I got started.

Some time ago I found myself lonely at heart. I needed to add some excitement to my life and meet new friends. So I made a plan of action. First I created a seven-course appetizer menu, including a mai tai punch. Next, I made up a charming little flyer (total cost: $1.50) with the menu, directions, map, and phone number. The headline read something like: "Knowing that you are very special, you are invited to a gourmet seduction and a meeting with other special people."

For four evenings I went around town and every time I saw an appealing single lady, I just approached her saying, "Hi, my name is Jacques. You look like a person who likes to have a good time and meet new people. Here is a personal invitation just for you. Take my word for it, it is the best place in town for gourmet seduction. Bye for now, I must run to a meeting." Did it work? But of course!

By Friday, I had given out 50 flyers. So here comes Saturday night. I invited four of my good male friends to share the evening. Guess what? By 8:30 p.m., there were seventeen gorgeous ladies digging into my gourmet appetizers, sipping *z'punch*, dancing, and talking. We had a blast! And I asked my guests to add their names and phone numbers to my guest book, so they would all get invited to the next party. Well, that took care of my loneliness. I became very popular instantly. The words "gourmet seduction" are magic. It worked for me, and I am sure it will work for you.

Lonely at Heart

Menu 5

Two dozen roses

Appetizers for approximately 20 people:

Shrimps Zucchini

Lobster Toasts

Ginger Beef Sticks

Sesame Drumettes and Wings

Checkerboard Caviar

Assorted Fruits and Cheese

Cocktails and Mai Tai Punch

Red Burgundy, Chablis and Blush Rose Wines

Shrimps Zucchini

Wash **4 whole fresh zucchini** and cut in half lengthwise.

Mix and refrigerate for 30 minutes:

      1 pound cooked bay shrimps

      1 cup diced celery

      4 ounces Parmesan cheese

      1/8 cup mayonnaise

      1 teaspoon dry mustard

      1/4 teaspoon seafood seasoning

Spoon out center of zucchini as deep as possible without piercing skin. Fill center with shrimp mixture. Refrigerate. Just before serving, cut zucchini in about 1-inch long slices. Display on platter. Decorate with parsley branches and slices of **2 lemons**.

Lobster Toast

Steam or boil **1 12-ounce lobster tail** for about 8 minutes.

Remove shell.
Clean membranes from lobster.
Chop lobster as finely as possible.

Then mix lobster meat with:
> **1/2 pound grated Swiss cheese**
> **2 ounces butter**
> **1/4 teaspoon seafood seasoning**

Spread mixture evenly on **10 slices toasted white bread**.
Place on baking sheet.
Sprinkle with **paprika**. Broil 3 minutes.

Cut lobster toast in triangular shapes.
Display on a large platter.
Cut in half lengthwise:
> **8 ounces canned pitted black canned olives**

Place them on individual toasts and serve.

Ginger Beef Sticks

Ask your butcher to slice approximately **2-1/2 pounds flank beef** very thin across grain.

Peel and mince:

3 tablespoons fresh ginger roots

Put in bowl with:

1/2 cup chopped scallion

1/4 cup soy sauce

2 tablespoons sugar

Add beef and mix thoroughly. Refrigerate for 3 hours. Take out beef strips. Cut in half. Skew on extra long toothpicks. Broil about 8 to 10 minutes. Place on a platter and serve.

Sesame Drumettes and Wings

Cut **3 pounds chicken wings** and **small chicken drumsticks** (drumettes) into 3 pieces each and discard tips.

Mix together:

> **1/2 cup prepared mustard**
>
> **1/2 cup raw honey**

Coat drumettes and wings and coat well with mixture. Place them on a baking sheet.

Sprinkle with:

> **1/4 pound sesame seeds**

Bake in 350° oven approximately 25 minutes. Check oven after 20 minutes. If chicken is dark golden brown, it is ready. Place on platter to serve.

Checkerboard Caviar

Have at hand:

> 1 3-ounce jar red caviar
>
> 1 3-ounce jar black caviar
>
> 10 slices toasted bread
>
> 8 ounces cream cheese
>   (take out of refrigerator
>   45 minutes ahead of time)

Spread cheese over each toast. Spread 5 toasts semi-heavily with red caviar and 5 with black caviar. Cut toast into 4 square pieces. On a large tray place one red square toast and one black so it looks like a checkerboard. Serve.

Assorted Fruits and Cheese

Core and slice:

> **3 delicious apples**
>
> **3 golden pears**

Squeeze juice of **one lemon** into large mixing bowl. Add the apple and pear slices and mix thoroughly. This will prevent fruit from turning brown.

Wash and prepare:

> **1-1/2 pounds red seedless grapes**
>
> **1-1/2 pounds green seedless grapes**
>
> **2 quarts fresh strawberries**

Display fruit on large platter with pieces of:

> **8 ounces French Camembert or Brie cheese**
>
> **8 ounces Swiss cheese**
>
> **8 ounces Gouda cheese**

Heat **1 long baguette French bread**. Slice bread about 1/2-inch thick and display around fruit and cheese on platter. Serve.

Mai Tai Punch

For one individual drink, mix:

> 1 ounce light rum
> 1 ounce dark rum
> 3 ounces each pineapple and orange juices
> 1 ounce grenadine

Pour over crushed ice in a 10-ounce glass.

To decorate each drink, place together onto a skewer:

> 1 slice of fresh orange
> 1 chunk of pineapple
> 1 maraschino cherry

Cut a small slit in orange slice. Place skewer in rim of glass. Serve.

To make Mai Tai Punch, increase the above ingredients by 10; mix in a large, attractive punch bowl. (See Résumé, next page, for a tip on keeping the Punch cold.)

RÉSUMÉ

$\mathcal{D}$oes this sound like fun? But of course! This gourmet seduction is very easy. Everything can be prepared in advance, except the mai tai punch, because you may be tempted to drink it all.

Here is a tip on *z'punch*. Fill 2 sandwich-size ziplock plastic bags with water. Freeze them overnight. After you make your punch, put just one bag of frozen ice (at a time) into the punchbowl. It works better than ice, which dissolves and dilutes the quality of *z'punch*, you know.

Use imagination when displaying your food—be artistic. The eye appeal is very important. I personally like a white tablecloth and some green foliage between platters of food. Set the romantic mood with music, candles, dimmed lights, cats and dogs outside. You know, some ladies may be allergic to cats and really don't want any animals jumping up on them and their outfits.

Be sure either you or one of your friends acts as host and greets each lady with a rose when she arrives. Don't forget, this is the best time to ask her to sign the guest book. Then make sure that everyone is introduced to each other. It helps to break *z'ice*, you know. From here on, it is up to you and your friends to keep the party going.

One word of advice: Circulate among your guests. Ladies don't like to be ignored, you know. Establishing communication is point number one of this gourmet seduction. I have learned it is best to spend some time with each lady guest to establish the interest to meet again. It is better to have the chance of seven or eight dates in the future than to put all your eggs in one basket. I remember once spending half the evening romanc-

ing a tall, blonde beauty, only to learn at 11:30 p.m. that she had to leave to pick up her fiance! Truly, my loss—she was so lovely and I missed my chance to meet all the others! Also, I believe ladies are more intrigued when a gentleman does not ask for a date on their first meeting—it leaves them to guess why you didn't, and creates mystery.

Believe, and it will work for you. Be patient! You can use *z'art* of gourmet seduction any time you need to. See you again. *A Bientot.*

Great Expectations

*H*ow many times, my friends, have we said to ourselves with great expectations, "I must do this thing or that"? We get excited about the idea or situation, and daydream about this new adventure. We ask ourselves, "Should I do it or not?" Some will spend their whole lives debating that question. Some will never do it, but years later will admit, "I should have." But not me! A Gemini, equipped with a vivid imagination and a quest for adventure, I decide quickly and then I make it happen.

I owned a gourmet cooking school in Florida several years ago. During dinner with a friend one night, he showed me a handful of real gold nuggets that he had mined in the jungles of Columbia, South America. Guess what? I got gold fever, you know. So I decided I would try my hand at gold mining and jungle survival. I even became "a man without a country" for several days! Listen to this experience…

I am so excited about going on this adventure, I don't notice that my Canadian visa is not returned to me at the airline counter. I arrive in Calle, Columbia and the immigration officer says, "Where is your visa?" Ho! I do not have it. I give *z'customs* officer a $100 bill and say, "Please make necessary arrangements to get it here, and keep the change." Wrong! He

says "I'm sorry, but I cannot do that." Even *por favor, senor* does not work. "No sweat," I say. "I will take the next plane back to get it." Wrong again! *Z'plane* does not fly back for four days. They give me just enough time to grab my suitcase and escort me back to *z'plane*. So I tell my friends, "Don't worry. I'll catch up with you in a day or so." Wrong again! *Z'plane* takes off and lands in Peru. Boy, I will be so happy to get off *z'plane* and make different traveling arrangements. Ho! Wrong again! They will not even let me off *z'plane* without a visa. After waiting five hours in *z'plane* (while it is cleaned and refueled), we take off. So I think, "In the next country, I will get off." Wrong again!

After repeating this scene several times, I begin to look the way I smell. I finally get to Santiago, Chile—dead tired (I could not sleep in *z'plane*). So I am allowed to get off and go to a hotel. I sleep until 10:30 p.m. I get up and open my suitcase to shower, shave and change my clothes. Wrong again! I had grabbed the wrong suitcase—one that belonged to my female traveling companion. It is very hot and humid. There is no air conditioning. I decide instead to go for a walk. The streets are empty—I find it very unusual that no one else is out walking about. Suddenly I hear running footsteps, so I stick my head out around the corner of the building. The first thing I see is the barrel of a machine gun—it looked like a cannon! The soldier holding it says something I cannot understand. I stick my hands way up in the air, and break out into a cold sweat—I could hardly breathe. Next, I am parading in *z'square* with this gun in my back. I end up in the *palacio* where the jail is, then shortly after I am taken back to *z'hotel*. I did not know there was a curfew and the police had orders to shoot on sight anyone out after the curfew! Well, there's more, but I will not go on-and-on. This is *Z'Art of Gourmet Seduction*, not a novel, you know.

I reunited with my friends and headed for the jungle. We arrived in Barbacos, the last semi-civilized trading post, where we slept in a shack on *z'floor*. Next we traveled 14 hours by canoe on the Petilla River, full of whirlpools and logs coming at

us constantly. By nightfall, we entered *z'Non Salve River*, which was calm but strange—like canoeing in a dark tunnel with tree branches sticking out all around. I thought it was rather romantic, until I learned it was it was full of snakes!

The music of *z'jungle* creatures was quite entertaining. When we missed our campsite in the dark, we were asked to sing along so that our engineers could hear us, and guide us to the camp. When we finally arrived, I got out of the canoe only to realize a huge frog with sucker toes was hugging my thigh! Ho! What's this?

Well, we survived in the jungle for three months, living off the *z'fruits* of the land and water. I returned in one piece, without any gold, but with one heck of an adventure to remember which I am mostly happy to have experienced (except for that frog!).

Don't forget—we all live in some sort of jungle. So why not try your hand at *z'next* gourmet seduction and see if you will enter into your own adventure? Go for it—especially with "great expectations."

Great Expectations

Menu 6

One Rose

Tomato Farcie au Fromage

Belgian Endive au Beurre D'Amandes

Red Snapper Papillotte

Fresh Green Beans with Lemon Butter and Pomme
D'Ores

Banana au Pernod

White or Rose Wine

Tomato Farcie au Fromage

Wash **1 large tomato** and cut it in half. Empty both centers completely. Save tomato meat but discard seeds.

Chop very finely:

> **1 green bell pepper**

Mix with:

> **2 ounces Muenster cheese, grated**

Fill centers of tomato halves. Then mix together:

> **1 ounce bread crumbs**
>
> **2 tablespoons butter**

Spread on each tomato half. Sprinkle lightly with paprika. Bake in 375° oven for 20 minutes. Serve over a **lettuce leaf**.

Belgian Endives au Beurre D'Amandes

Wash **2 endives** and cut in half.

In a frying pan, heat:
>   **3 ounces butter (3/4 stick)**

Cook endives 3 minutes on medium heat on the flat side. Remove and set aside.

Then grind:
>   **2 ounces almonds**

Add to butter drippings in frying pan and season with:
>   **juice of 1 lime**
>   **salt and pepper**

Cook 2 minutes. Spoon over endives. Serve.

Red Snapper Papillotte

Place **2 8-ounce fresh red snapper** on 2 sheets of foil paper large enough to fold and seal.

Spread evenly on fillets:

> **2 ounces butter (1/2 stick)**
>
> **4 tablespoons white wine**

Top fillets with:

> **1/4 cup chopped scallions**
>
> **1/4 cup chopped red bell pepper**
>
> **2 tablespoons chopped parsley**
>
> **1/2 teaspoon seafood seasoning**

Seal foil tightly in a dome shape. Place on baking sheet. Bake in 375° oven for 18 minutes. If fillets are too thick, you may have to bake an extra 2 to 3 minutes. Snapper should be moist and flake easily with fork when done. Serve.

Green Beans with Lemon Butter

Wash and trim **3/4 pound fresh green beans**. Cook in steamer for 12 to 15 minutes until tender, but firm.

In small saucepan melt:

> **2 ounces butter (1/2 stick)**

Add:

> **juice of one lemon**
>
> **salt and pepper**

Cook for 2 minutes. Spoon over beans. Use **lemon slices** for decoration for snapper, along with **parsley**. Serve.

Banana au Pernod

Peel **2 medium bananas** and slice in about 1-inch thick slices. In large frying pan over medium heat, place **3 ounces butter (3/4 stick)**. Fry banana pieces on both sides.

Then add:

1 ounce pernod

Stand back and ignite. Cook 1 minute. Remove banana and spoon over:

6 ounces vanilla ice cream

Add to frying pan:

3 tablespoons powdered sugar

2 ounces pernod

Cook 2 minutes. Pour sauce over bananas and ice cream. Serve.

Pomme D'Ores

Peel **2 large baking potatoes**. Make small balls with melon scoop (if not available, cut into small 1/2-inch squares).

In a very hot frying pan, heat **3 ounces olive oil**. Add potatoes. Keep moving them around while cooking until golden brown, about 15 to 18 minutes. Remove.

Pat dry to remove excess oil. Salt and pepper to taste. Serve.

RÉSUMÉ

*W*ell, my friend, you thought I was going to suggest a jungle gourmet seduction? Not so.

The variety of foods we ate while in the jungle was limited. But I had my imagination! I learned to do a lot more with bananas than the monkeys do—I can even peel them faster. We collected much of our own food—bananas, lemons, wild fruits and vegetables, and I cut hearts of palm daily. Fish were plentiful. A friendly native tribe came on Sundays to trade. They were most interested in trading eggs and wild chickens for our clothes. I traded my jeans for a big skinny chicken which I boiled for five hours, but still it was like rubber. But the broth was good.

This gourmet seduction could be used for a wild lady of your choice, or perhaps when you are invited to go on safari, you know. The menu is easy to prepare. Just follow the instructions. Don't overcook the snapper; it will get tough. If you like, you may serve the Pernod (a licorice liqueur, like absinthe) as a cocktail: 2 ounces of pernod over ice and add 3 ounces of water. Or add 2 ounces to after-dinner coffee or, serve it just over ice. But don't drink too much Pernod! You may wake up in *z'jungle* if you do!

If you feel really adventurous, set *z'table* outside, weather permitting. Play some Harry Belafonte; light some Venetian or marine candles (these are best outside if it's a bit windy). Your great expectations for your gourmet seduction may be right on target! *Bonne chance. A Bientot.*

Spices and Love

Spices and love—they make the perfect pair, you know. Remember your very first kiss? Did you find it sweet and spicy? But of course you did! And surely you remember your first Mexican hot tamale. I bet they both made you blush.

I am certain you know a really spicy young lady who is ready for a spicy gourmet seduction. Let me tell you about one I met.

I was in Piccadilly Square in London while vacationing in England. I didn't know a soul there and was having lunch alone in a pub. I don't remember much about the meal except that there was a most delicious young lady sitting across the room. I could not take my eyes away from her, you know. When we finally made eye contact, I gave her a big smile which she returned. I asked the server if she knew that young lady. She said, "Her? Oh, don't bother. She's weird. . .too strange."

I decided anyway to see if I could break *z'ice*. On my way out, I stopped for a second, turned around, walked straight to her table and said, "*Bonjour, Mademoiselle*. I believe that I owe you an apology." She looked at me and asked why. "Because I am guilty of losing control of my eyes."

She replied quickly, "You are a French Canadian, aren't you?"

"But of course. How did you know?"

Her reply was, "I just know."

I laughed, and then she asked, "May I offer you another gin and tonic?"

I answered, "Why? So I can go back home with the satisfaction of having shared a cocktail with *z'most* delicious young lady in England? May I sit down?"

After 30 minutes of conversation (about gourmet seductions, of course), I found myself carrying grocery bags into her magnificent cottage—all the fixings for a spicy gourmet seduction. I missed my plane back home twice.

This gourmet seduction represents my memory of this splendid British lady. Weird she was not. Spicy? But of course!

S*pices and* L*ove*

Menu 7

One rose

Smoked Salmon aux Capres

Bib Lettuce Roquefort

Steak Diablo

Asparagus Bearnaise

Stuffed Potato

Raspberry Flan

Red Burgundy or Cabernet Wine

Smoked Salmon aux Capres

Have on hand:

4 ounces smoked salmon (lox)

2 ounces cream cheese

2 ounces capers

1 lemon

dash of cayenne pepper

Drain capers. Spread cream cheese on each layer of salmon. Sprinkle with pepper. Place some capers on each. Roll salmon. Refrigerate. Before serving, cut into small portions. Place on top of **lettuce leaves**. Cut lemon in half to decorate. Serve.

Bib Lettuce Roquefort

Wash, break, and refrigerate:

> **1 head of bib lettuce**

In saucepan place:

> **2 ounces olive oil**

Warm over medium heat. Add:

> **juice of 2 limes**
>
> **1 tablespoon sugar**
>
> **1/2 teaspoon each salt and pepper**

Add, stirring constantly:

> **2 ounces Roquefort (bleu) cheese**

When smooth, pour sauce over lettuce, mix and serve with 1-ounce of cheese bits on top of each salad.

Steak Diablo

Mix in blender until powdery:

> **1 tablespoon each red chili pepper and**
> **black pepper**
> **1 teaspoon rosemary**
> **1 bay leaf**
> **1/8 teaspoon garlic powder**

Add and blend two minutes:

> **2 ounces olive oil**

Prepare **2 12-ounce New York strip steaks**. Trim all fat and gristle. Pour mixture from blender over steak in a plastic sealable container. Turn steaks 3 or 4 times. Press on container lid. Refrigerate for 24 hours. Take steaks out 1 hour before cooking.

In a cast iron or thick frying pan, heat:

> **2 ounces butter (1/2 stick)**

Heat until butter is smoking (start your exhaust fan). Cook steaks to your taste (medium rare is best), approximately 3 minutes on each side. Remove steaks and keep warm.

Add to pan:

> **4 tablespoons of marinade**
>
> **4 ounces red wine**

Cook 5 minutes. Then add to sauce:

> **2 tablespoons each soy sauce and steak**
> **sauce**

Reduce sauce by one third volume. Place steaks in sauce. Cook 1 minute on both sides. Place steaks on platters. Spoon 2 tablespoons sauce on each, decorate with vegetables. Serve.

Asparagus Bearnaise

Trim and wash **1 pound fresh asparagus**. Steam for about 12 minutes until tender. Keep warm.

Mix together:

> **1/8 cup tarragon vinegar**
>
> **1 teaspoon tarragon leaves**

Let stand for 20 minutes. In double boiler, melt:

> **1/4 pound butter**

Transfer to a cup and set aside. Put into double boiler:

> **4 egg yolks**
>
> **1/4 teaspoon dry mustard**

Keep stirring constantly. Remove from burner and slowly add butter, 1 tablespoon at a time. Repeat until it gets very thick. Add 1 tablespoon of the tarragon vinegar and leaves. Keep stirring rapidly. Repeat until all ingredients are used. Do not use liquid on the bottom of butter cup. Discard. Keep beating sauce.
Add:

> **1/4 cup minced parsley**
>
> **1/2 teaspoon tabasco sauce**

Refrigerate 20 minutes. Serve 2 tablespoons on top of each serving of hot asparagus.

Stuffed Potato

Bake **1 extra large baking potato** in 400° oven for approximately 45 minutes. Cut potato in half lengthwise.

Spoon out meat and mash together with:

> **1 egg**
> **2 tablespoons butter**
> **2 tablespoons grated Parmesan cheese**
> **salt and pepper**

Refill potato skins. Bake in 475° oven, on top shelf, for approximately 15 minutes.

Raspberry Flan

Beat together:

> **4 eggs**
>
> **1/2 cup sugar**

Add:

> **2 cups milk**

Beat 1 minute and sprinkle with salt. Pour mixture into two custard dishes. Place in hot water in baking pan. Bake at 325° for approximately 1 hour, until center of flan is solid. Insert a small knife into center. If knife comes out clean, flan is ready. Remove from oven and cool for 30 minutes. Refrigerate for 2 hours.

Put into a blender:

> **1 pint red raspberries (Frozen, if not in season. Reserve a dozen for decoration.)**
>
> **1 ounce brandy**

Beat for 3 minutes at high speed. Cook in a saucepan for 15 minutes over medium heat, or until it looks like syrup. Pass through a fine mesh sieve. Refrigerate for 1 hour.

To unmold flan, carefully run a knife around the entire outside edge of the custard dish. Invert the serving plate on top of the custard dish. Holding the plate and dish firmly together, turn them upside down; give a couple of little shakes, and the flan will slide out of the dish onto the plate.

Pour 3 tablespoons raspberry sauce over the flan. Decorate with reserved raspberries.

RÉSUMÉ

*T*have found that there is a spice that compares to every woman. This is why spices are so important to *z'art* of gourmet seduction. When I first created my gourmet seductions, I experimented a lot. Ah—the spice of life! It is exciting and very rewarding. I have been fortunate to be able to travel to many different countries, sampling new spices and perfecting my gourmet seductions.

I am always searching for new love and new spices. All spices have their own distinct pigment, taste, form, and associations. Much like men and women, a perfect combination is necessary to obtain *z'perfect* balance.

Each of us has wondered at time why life must be so limited, no? Well, I finally learned that we put our own limitations on everything we experience. I remember my father saying to me, "Son, you may be a tumbleweed for most of your life, but it is much better than being a totem pole." So if you feel like tumbling a little—if you're tired of the same old thing—get out of *z'rut!* Go search for your perfect mixture of love and spices. Try *z'art* of gourmet seduction. It will spice up your love life.

This gourmet seduction is really easy. So you do not need me to lead you by the hand and show you how. Be confident and do it all by yourself! That is *z'spice* of gourmet seduction. *A Bientot.*

Divorce by Candlelight

$\mathcal{I}$s 'divorce' a nasty word? But of course. It doesn't have to be though. In the early '40s in my native country, Canada, divorce was almost a crime. I remember people being chased out of small towns because they were divorcing. Our society has changed its attitudes about divorce but regrettably, it seems to have become a way of life in our society.

I believe most divorces happen because there is a break-down in the communication between a couple. Since each one of us is in a constant process of evolution, our relationships are bound to change as we do. I am certain when two people fall in love and get married they do not anticipate divorce.

But I ask myself, how can the love that keeps two people together for years turn so suddenly, sometimes, to hate? Is it better for a married couple to continue living together with hate and misery, or to go their separate ways? "Until death us do part" makes no sense to me if the love has gone.

If people have decided to divorce it doesn't matter if the commitment has lasted a month or 50 years. There could be so many reasons for it—one's mind has expanded, and there is need for a change, or one has the need to experience life in

another direction, or one feels they still need to find their soulmate, or twin soul.

Whatever the reason, why make it nasty? Of course there is hurt in all divorces, but why let it turn to hate? If communication is open, why can't two mature persons sit down by candlelight—a gourmet seduction—and talk about their differences, and their individual needs and wants, in a civilized way?

Why not talk about your plans in a most romantic way—with a different kind of gourmet seduction? Begin with the lighting of two candles as a symbol of the fire of love that brought you together (and that still may be flickering), even if you agree that the only way to happiness is on separate paths. Share your memories of all the best moments you shared together. If, by the fifth course, you decide to change your mind about divorce, realize that you have just experienced the ultimate gourmet seduction! Whether you save your marriage, or choose divorce and the evening helps you part as friends, don't you think the evening was worth it? But of course!

$\mathcal{D}$*ivorce by* $\mathcal{C}$*andlelight*

Menu 8

One yellow rose and one red rose

Petongle d'Amour

Salad Pinky

Coco Shrimps

Rice au Legumes

Kiwi Flambe

White Pouilly Fuisse

Petongle d'Amour

Wash **1/2 pound large scallops** and slice twice across the grain.

Put into a large frying pan over medium heat:

> **8 ounces clam juice**
>
> **1/2 teaspoon seafood seasoning**
>
> **dash of salt**

Simmer for 5 minutes. Add scallops. Poach for 4 minutes. Take out scallops and set aside. Reduce broth by one half.

Then add:

> **2 ounces sweet sherry**

Cook two minutes and set aside. In a saucepan over medium heat, melt:

> **1 tablespoon butter**

Add: **1 tablespoon flour**

Cook one minute. Keep stirring. Add the clam broth. Cook 3 minutes more.

Then add:

> **2 egg yolks**
>
> **4 ounces fresh whipping cream**

Keep stirring and add:

> **1 tablespoon paprika**

Cook 1 minute more. Remove from burner. Put scallops in two individual-sized baking casseroles. Pour sauce over scallops. Place under broiler for 3 minutes and serve.

Salad Pinky

Wash **1 head of red leaf lettuce**, break into pieces and then refrigerate.

Into a small deep container, put:

> **2 egg yolks**
>
> **1/4 teaspoon dry mustard**

Beat for 1 minute with electric hand beater. Then slowly add:

> **3 ounces olive oil**

Drain and put into blender:

> **2 ounces red beets in natural juice**

Add to beets:

> **juice of 1 lemon**
>
> **dash of salt and cayenne pepper**

Blend until smooth and add to dressing, a little at a time. Continue beating until smooth. Refrigerate until ready to serve over lettuce.

Coco Shrimps

Peel and devein and then refrigerate:

> **3/4 pound large shrimps**

Break apart and save milk from:

> **1 fresh coconut**

Blend or grate coconut meat as finely as possible. Dry coconut in 300° oven until light brown. Set aside.

Melt **1 tablespoon butter** in a small saucepan. Add **1 tablespoon flour**, stirring constantly. Cook for 1 minute.

Then add:

> **4 ounces of the coconut milk**

Beat together and add:

> **2 egg yolks**
>
> **3 ounces fresh whipping cream**

Season with:

> **pinch of seafood seasoning**
>
> **dash of salt**

Cook 5 minutes, then add:

> **1 ounce rum**

Remove from burner and set aside. Now, have at hand, along with the coconut milk mixture, the coconut and the shrimp:

> **4 ounces flour**

Roll each shrimp in flour, dip in milk, then in coconut. Place shrimps on a baking sheet. Bake in 350° oven, on middle shelf, approximately 15 minutes. Watch so shrimp doesn't get too dark brown. Serve with sauce over and decorate with one petal from each rose.

Rice au Legumes

In frying pan over medium heat, place **1 ounce sesame or coconut oil**.

Add and cook for 2 minutes:

> **1/2 cup sliced mushrooms**
>
> **1/4 cup chopped scallions**
>
> **1/4 cup chopped red bell peppers**
>
> **dash of salt and pepper**

Then add to vegetables and spices:

> **1 cup cooked rice**

Cook for 5 minutes, moving rice around so it does not stick or burn. Serve with entree.

Kiwi Flambe

Peel and slice crosswise **2 kiwi fruit.**

Melt **2 ounces butter (1/2 stick)** in frying pan over medium heat.

Add the kiwi slices and cook for 2 minutes.

Pour on, stand back, and ignite:

> **1 ounce brandy**

Remove kiwi slices.

Add to syrup:

> **2 tablespoons powdered sugar**
> **2 ounces orange liqueur**

Arrange kiwi slices over **2 4-ounce servings of orange sorbet.** Pour sauce over kiwi and serve.

RÉSUMÉ

Z'most important thing to remember about this gourmet seduction is your goal—do you want a divorce or do you want to try to save your marriage? Well, my friend, the chances are 50-50, it could go either way.

Remember to talk only about all the best times you have shared together. At all costs, stay away from the bad experiences! You may feel like a rat at first, but things will change gradually during the evening. You may even share a few tears, you know. Yes, macho men can cry. Just try to keep glued together, and be a gentleman, even if it is painful.

Express how life is difficult to understand at times. Proceed gently. Take a step back by saying something like, "You know, my darling, I need your help. Tell me why it is so difficult for us to make it. Where did I go wrong? We sure don't deserve to have this happen to us. Please forgive me for any hurt I may have caused you, my love." You must sound convincing enough to keep your lady calm. Chances are if you use this approach, she will react by blaming herself for the breakdown. Don't let her accept the blame—explain that it is not one person's fault. Say nothing to upset her. Allow your lady to retain, or regain, her composure.

You have made your points (and your decision), so don't keep talking about it. Instead, I suggest that you two spend the rest of this gourmet seduction in a romantic way, perhaps say, "My love, would you do me the honor of this dance?" This will help to end the evening on a positive note. For whatever reason you may divorce, do whatever you can to keep hatred from entering your hearts.

Why two roses? you are wondering, no? Well, as I said, no one knows how the evening could turn out. Say that by dessert, you feel that divorce is the only way. Then reach over and give to your lady *z'yellow* rose, which, for me, represents cheerful separation. If you have decided to give it another try, then give your lady *z'red* rose, and eat *z'yellow* rose!

I truly hope that my gourmet seduction, "Divorce by Candlelight," can help you create a more civilized way of separating, or reuniting!

I could stay to help you with this gourmet seduction, but I feel this can be handled only between you and your lady. Besides, I am a sucker for tears, you know. Who needs a threesome tear-jerker party anyway? Good luck. *A Bientot.*

Body and Soul

It is fun to use *z'art* of gourmet seduction and sample the good life. However, it is not the complete answer. Do I enjoy meeting *z'beautiful* ladies? But of course! Being a romantic, as I am, I find it very fulfilling. But most honestly, my friend, I feel there is something important missing. Does that sound familiar?

Not long ago, my adventurous life took me to Gabon, Africa. I had accepted a job to be a food consultant for an oil drilling operation. As I reclined one night on the helicopter's landing deck, atop an oil-drilling barge, looking at millions of stars above me, I asked myself, "What am I doing here?" My answer was that I needed to spend some one-on-one time with my soul, to re-evaluate what was missing. I realized the missing element was true love—someone to trust and share my life, body and soul. In other words, I needed to find Ms. Right.

Love is more important to our fulfillment than many people will admit. The search to find the perfect person with whom to spend our life can seem never-ending. When you think about it, it is no easy task! I know that there is someone here on earth that can fulfill my dream and share my life in every way—with true love and happiness.

I quickly realized that an oil-drilling barge off the coast of Africa was probably not *z'place* to find my body and soul mate! So before long, I was back in the good old USA. (How good it feels to step on the soil of home again! It is amazing how much more you appreciate home when you get away from it.)

Back at my headquarters in Orlando, Florida, I had a feeling that something very positive would soon happen to me. Well, many positive things have happened, and I have hosted many memorable gourmet seductions. But, my search continues for Ms. Right, you know.

Meanwhile, my friends, this gourmet seduction is one of my favorites. So feel comfortable and secure with it. You may discover your soul mate with this one!

Body and Soul

Menu 9

One Rose

Champignons Farcis aux Huitres

Butter Lettuce with Feta Dressing

Veal Neptune

Bouquet de Legumes

Glace D'Amaretto

One half bottle champagne Moet Chandon

One half bottle Rose D'Anjou

Champignons Farcis aux Huitres

Clean and remove part of center from **6 large mushroom caps.**

Blanch mushroom caps for 5 minutes in water (enough to cover) over high heat with **1/2 teaspoon salt** added. Drain and set aside.

Pry open and remove shells from:

> **6 fresh oysters**

In saucepan over medium heat, melt:

> **1 ounce butter**

Add oysters, cook for 1 minute then add:

> **juice of 1 lime**
>
> **pinch of seafood seasoning**

Cook 1 minute. Remove from burner. Take out oysters. Put one on each mushroom cap.

To drippings in pan add:

> **2 tablespoons bread crumbs**

Mix well and divide into 6 parts. Pack the top of each cap with mixture. Sprinkle with **paprika**. Broil for 5 minutes. Do not let them get too brown. Serve.

Butter Lettuce with Feta Dressing

Wash **1 head butter lettuce**, break into pieces, and re-frigerate.

Chop into small squares and set aside:

> **3 ounces feta cheese**

Mix in saucepan over medium heat:

> **2 ounces olive oil**
>
> **1 ounce wine vinegar**
>
> **juice of 1 lemon**
>
> **2 tablespoons sugar**
>
> **1/4 teaspoon each salt and pepper**

Cook for 3 minutes then add:

> **the prepared feta cheese**
>
> **2 tablespoons chopped ripe olives**

Remove from burner. Let cool for 30 minutes. Refrig-erate for 30 minutes. Pour over lettuce just before serv-ing.

Veal Neptune

Prepare **2 12-ounce thick veal chops** by inserting sharp knife on the meaty side of chops and making pockets.

Mix together and stuff chops with:

> **2 ounces fresh crab meat (well cleaned)**
> **2 ounces grated Swiss cheese**

Fill as tightly as possible and secure with toothpicks. Then, in large frying pan over high heat, melt **2 ounces butter**. Brown chops on both sides. Place in 350° oven for 25 minutes.

Now add to drippings:

> **2 ounces port wine**
> **juice of 1 lemon**

Cook 5 minutes, then add:

> **1/4 cup fresh whipping cream**
> **tarragon leaves**
> **pinch of salt and pepper**

Stir until smooth. Pour over chops and serve.

Bouquet de Legumes

Clean, trim, and peel these vegetables:

1/4 pound asparagus

1 large carrot

3 ounces green beans

Cut carrots lengthwise, very thin. Put them first into steamer, then add the green beans, and top with the asparagus. Steam for approximately 12 to 15 minutes. When asparagus is done, so are other veggies.

Then broil and remove the skin from:

1 small red bell pepper

Cut in half crosswise. Cut 1/2-inch off top and bottom. Artistically arrange vegetables through pepper rings, to resemble a "bouquet."

Mix together and pour over veggies:

1 ounce melted butter

pinch of salt and pepper

Serve with entree.

Glace D'Amaretto

Put into mixer:

8 ounces almond ice cream

(if not available, vanilla will do)

Add:

2 ounces amaretto liqueur

Beat 20 seconds on slow speed.

Pour into coupé or margarita glasses. Freeze for one hour.

Pour **1 ounce additional amaretto** over top.

Top with **maraschino cherries** and serve.

RÉSUMÉ

$\mathcal{M}$y friends, in my search for Ms. Right, I must have prepared this gourmet seduction a dozen times. It has brought ecstasy to many of *z'most* beautiful ladies. Only one time it did not work out the way I planned. The lady was very late to arrive and somehow we instantly developed an appetite for something else, which has nothing to do with *z'menu*. But of course, she was given a second invitation, and the next time, she thoroughly enjoyed my gourmet seduction.

It is good that I enjoy preparing gourmet seductions, because after two years, Ms. Right is still a mystery. But I know in my heart that I will find her soon. And when she appears, I will know, body and soul, that she is the one.

I am sure that you will have all *z'luck* in the world with this gourmet seduction. By now you don't need me to help you, so go right ahead. Happy hunting! *A Bientot.*

Z'Electromagnetic Field of Love

Beware! This could happen to you. Have you ever entered the "Electromagnetic Field of Love?" After spending half your life searching for, let's say, your Cinderella, suddenly you are face-to-face with her. Your eyes lock onto hers, you are looking deep into her majestic soul. You feel the strong vibration of the Electromagnetic Field pulling you closer and closer towards her. Almost paralyzed and speechless, your heart is beating five hundred times per minute.

When this happens to you, don't panic. Regain your composure quickly, take one step back, and unlock your eyes. Now, slowly glance from her feet all the way up to her hair and softly say, "Unbelievable. . .I must be dreaming. . . The fantasy of my dreams is here, alive, right in front of me. Please forgive me. . .I am in shock. . . My name is. . ." Then extend your hand, grasp hers gently, slowly raise her hand up, and kiss it ever so lightly. She will probably tell you her name.

Quickly, in a humorous tone, relate your fantasy to her so you can explain your reaction of shock and amazement. Then move on to casual conversation and do your best to invite her for either lunch, cocktails, coffee, or dinner. Go for whatever is appropriate at that particular time of day. If you have a business

card, present it immediately. This creates a sense of trust. Above all, if possible, don't let her get away from you. Unleash all of your charm and charisma, but don't be pushy.

Assuming that you have succeeded with your invitation, gradually express your desire to create a very special gourmet dinner to celebrate the actual realization of your lifelong fantasy. Most ladies will be flattered by such an invitation; however, be very careful not to show your anxiety by suggesting a specific day. It is much safer to ask her what evening would be most appropriate. She will respond much more openly to this approach. If given the opportunity, you could suggest the earliest convenient evening.

Keep in mind this gourmet seduction could be the most important one you have ever prepared—you must become a Cinderella's prince. Be romantic, but above all, be a gentleman. You definitely have your mind set on winning your Cinderella's heart, but she will be evaluating you, so stay poised. Be cool and calm, and maybe your fantasy happiness will come true.

After you've reviewed each of the following recipes, let me advise you on how to proceed step-by-step, complete with some romantic poems and tips.

Z 'Electromagnetic Field of Love

Menu 10

One Dozen Roses—six pink and six red

Alaskan Bisque

Strawberries Floridian

Butterflies of Veal Cinderella

Wild Rice aux Champignons and Cherries of the Sea

Star Fruits Flambe

Champagne Dom Perignon

White Poulli Montrachet

Alaskan Bisque

In saucepan over medium heat, sauté **1 tablespoon minced shallots** in **1 tablespoon butter.**

Cook 1 minute, then add 1 tablespoon flour.

Stir and cook 2 minutes.

Then add, stir, and cook 7 minutes:

> **8 ounces clam juice**
>
> **pinch each of salt and seafood seasoning**

Mix together and add:

> **2 egg yolks**
>
> **4 ounces fresh whipping cream**

Cook 3 minutes. Then add **4 ounces Alaskan crabmeat** (completely remove all shell and cartilage from crabmeat). Cook 1 minute. Remove from burner and keep warm.

Meanwhile, peel **1 lime**, cut in half and slice paper thin. Dip one half each slice in **paprika** and one half in **chopped parsley.** Lay it gently on the center of the bowl of bisque. Serve.

Strawberries Floridian

Wash and clean **1 pint ripe strawberries**. Reserve one half. Thinly slice the remaining half.

Then put into blender:

>**2 egg yolks**
>
>**1/4 teaspoon dry mustard**

Beat at high speed for 1 minute then slowly add:

>**3 ounces almond oil**

Alternating with:

>**2 ounces fresh lemon juice**

Add the sliced strawberries and:

>**2 tablespoons sugar**
>
>**pinch of salt and pepper**

Beat 2 minutes and refrigerate.

Meanwhile, wash and clean **1 head iceburg lettuce**. Cut in half crosswise. Dismantle leaves from each portion, forming two "bird's nests."

Cut reserved strawberries in quarters and place into the center of lettuce nests. Pour dressing over and serve.

Butterflies of Veal Cinderella

Ask your butcher for **2 large thin slices of veal, 10-ounces young milk-fed veal scallop.** Trim and cut 4 large veal scallops into butterfly wings. Cut 2 large square pieces of veal to be stuffed and rolled into cylindrical shape for butterflies' bodies.

Then mix together:

> **4 ounces chopped, cooked Florida lobster meat (equals 1 3/4 pound Florida lobster)**
>
> **2 ounces French Brie cheese**
>
> **pinch of seafood seasoning**

Place mixture on the 2 square pieces of veal. Roll into shape. In large frying pan over high heat melt 2 ounces butter. Quickly brown meat on both sides of wings and all sides of body. Place veal on a sheet pan and assemble into butterflies.

Decorate wings with:

> **6 small green stuffed olives, sliced**
>
> **6 small pitted black olives, sliced**
>
> **Set aside. Add to frying pan:**
>
> **2 ounces brandy**
>
> **1/4 cup beef bouillon**
>
> **pinch of salt and pepper**

Reduce by half. Then add:

1 ounce ham meat glaze (red)

Cook for 5 minutes or until it looks like light syrup. Spoon 2 tablespoons sauce over veal. Broil for 2 minutes. Do not let it change color. Remove from broiler. Display butterfly on each plate. Spoon out 2 more tablespoons of sauce on top, evenly but lightly. Break twigs of **parsley** to make 4 little antennae; arrange them around butterflies' heads. Serve with rice and veggies.

Wild Rice aux Champignons

Melt in frying pan over medium heat:
2 ounces butter (1/2 stick)

Add and cook for 5 minutes:
1 cup sliced fresh mushrooms
pinch of salt and pepper

Add and cook for 5 minutes:
1 cup cooked wild rice

Serve.

Cherries of the Sea

Wash and remove stems from **1 pint cherry tomatoes**. Select 6 large ones. Cut 1/3 off the top of each. With a small knife empty centers. Do not pierce skins.

Then mince and mix together:

> **3 ounces cooked bay shrimp**
>
> **1/4 cup grated Parmesan cheese**
>
> **paprika**

Fill centers of tomatoes. Bake in hot oven (400°) for 10 minutes.

Display them around rice next to butterfly and serve.

Star Fruits Flambe

Fill 2 margarita glasses with **3-ounce servings of lime sorbet**. Place in freezer for 15 minutes.

Wash and slice 1/8-inch thick:
2 star fruits

Remove small seeds. Discard 1/2-inch off both ends.

Then heat in large frying pan:
2 ounces butter (1/2 stick)

Cook star fruits on both sides for 8 minutes.

Then add:
1 ounce melon liqueur

Stand back and ignite. Cook 1 minute. Remove star fruits and place them on top of sorbets.

Add to frying pan:
2 ounces melon liqueur
2 tablespoons powdered sugar

Cook until it forms a heavy syrup. Pour over star fruits. Serve.

RÉSUMÉ

*W*ell, my dear friend, this is it—*Z-Big One*—your best performance. Remember, your first impression can be a winner or a loser, so don't guess. You must be very attentive. Read your script two or three times if you must. I have done this before and have been very successful.

First, call Cinderella a couple of days before your dinner is to take place. Through casual conversation, find out what her favorite foods are, such as seafood, veal, beef, poultry, etc. Chances are, this menu will be suitable, but if not, just select another from the choices in my book. Ask if she is allergic to certain foods, spices, or herbs. Ask about her wine preferences as well. Music is another important factor—be sure to work the conversation around to that. Cinderella will be taking notes about how sensitive you are to her needs. Let her know you are planning a romantic, candlelight dinner so she can dress appropriately. Make sure she understands it is not formal—no tux for you. A nice pair of slacks and crisp long-sleeve shirt will be fine. No necktie is necessary. Definitely no scented candles—they will kill all the beautiful cooking aromas.

Let's say that your dinner date will be arriving at 7:00 p.m. and dinner is at 8:00 p m You must begin preparations about 2:00 p.m. Do all your work ahead of time beginning with the wild rice. Add extra water if not fluffy enough. This can be reheated in the microwave before serving. Also prepare the bisque. This can be reheated later. Cut up all the ingredients for your salad and put into the serving bowl, but do not add your dressing until you are ready to serve. Keep the salad chilled. Prepare the vegetable, but bake only when preparing the entree. Assemble your veal but do not cook it until just before serving. The sauce can be prepared in advance. Place sweet (unsalted)

butter in your butter dish. For dessert, the fruit can be prepared ahead for the flambe. You can also make a good cappuccino or flavored coffee and offer a liqueur—melon is a good choice.

Okay, so far so good. Now you have some time to relax. Please stay sober, don't drink before she arrives. At 7:15 p.m. take one last spot check on all your efforts. Make sure the table is set properly. Water and wine glass in front. Butter plate and knife on the left. Salad forks in the freezer. Linen napkins folded butterfly shape in the center of the under (or charger) plate. Two candles in the center of the table, 11 roses on the center edge. Champagne glasses chilling in refrigerator. Ice bucket in kitchen. Selected music on, romantic dinner music ready to go. Soft lighting, but not too dark. If you have a fireplace, put some logs on to lend a soft glow to the room. Or if it is during the summer months, place several different-sized, unscented white candles in various-sized holders in the fireplace and light for a nice glowing "fire effect" with no heat.

$\mathcal{S}$tars in $\mathcal{M}$y $\mathcal{M}$ind

$\mathcal{A}$s you recall, my friends, I was in isolation at the North Pole for five years. My only connection to the civilized world was through pen pals, movies, and music. And I had my imagination and my dreams. There was one person, though, who made my life there more bearable. Music was very important to me. Everyday and night, I played all the albums of superstar recording artist, Connie Francis—a young Italian girl with a golden voice who sang her songs with so much feeling. Playing nothing else, I admit that I drove my whole staff crazy. However, no one could say too much; I was in charge, you know.

One day the movie, "Where the Boys Are", was shown. Guess who was z'star? The one and only, Connie Francis! After seeing the movie at least ten times, I created this far-fetched fantasy dream that someday I wanted to express my gratitude to Connie, with a most unique gourmet seduction—for saving me from going bananas up there.

Our fantasies rarely come true, right? Well, straight out of the blue, my fantasy did come true. Was it a case of being at the right place at the right time, or did it just take my subconscious mind that long to turn my fantasy into reality?

Whatever the reason, I picked up the phone not long ago, and guess who I was talking to? Connie Francis! Don't ask me if I was excited—I was floating in the air. After about 15 minutes of conversation, I expressed my profound desire to create in her honor an Expression of Love gourmet seduction. She said she appreciated that and was looking forward to enjoying my creation.

Do not think that gourmet seduction is used only for romancing—it is a powerful tool for establishing friendships, and business relationships, as well. I used *z'art* of gourmet seduction with my good friend Connie Francis only to express my gratitude. From that, we have developed a most respectable friendship. I am very proud to be among her friends.

I confess my great admiration for Connie. Believe me, she still can belt out a song like no one else.

My friends, *z'art* of gourmet seduction will work for you for any purpose, and everyone can do it. Stars in My Mind is probably one of my very best gourmet seductions.

$\mathcal{S}$*tars in* $\mathcal{M}$*y* $\mathcal{M}$*ind*

Menu 11

Antipasti
Gamberi alla Nettuno

Zuppa
Aragosta Bisquit con Sambuca

Insalata
Pomadori alla Giardiniera

Intermezzo
Gelato-Florida Stile

Piatta Principale
Vitello alla Frances con Verdura

Pasta Supreme
Dolce

Cuore di Amore
Espresso innaffiato con Licuore Frangelico

Buon appettito per *Concetta Frances*
da giacoma con amore,

Jacques Prudhomme

RÉSUMÉ

$\mathcal{I}$must share a secret with you, my friends. Because I am so grateful to Connie and her music for helping me to keep my sanity while I was in isolation for five years, I made a promise to her (and to myself) that I would never repeat this Italian gourmet seduction. So the recipes for Connie's gourmet seduction remain only with her.

I am forever thankful to Connie for providing me the opportunity to express my love and gratitude for all she has done for me. Connie has given enough of herself to millions of fans year-after-year. Her reward is knowing how many people, like me, have been filled with happiness by her touching and romantic voice.

From *z'bottom* of my heart, Connie—thank you!

Love and respect always,

Jacques

P.S. Extra Information to Help You

The following recipes are necessary for basic cooking. In order to make most sauces, you need some stock. When shopping, ask your butcher to give you 3 to 4 pounds of beef and veal bones. Also purchase a pound of beef short ribs.

Basic Brown Stock

Spread in a roasting pan:

> **3 to 4 pounds beef and veal bones**
>
> **1 pound beef short ribs**
>
> **1 cup chopped onions**
>
> **1 stalk celery, chopped**
>
> **1/2 cup diced carrots**

Bake at 400° until very brown. Drain off fat and save it. Pour everything else into a large kettle or pot.
Now add:

> **6 quarts water**
>
> **2 tablespoons salt**
>
> **2 bay leaves**
>
> **1 teaspoon black pepper**
>
> **1/2 teaspoon thyme**

Bring to a boil, reduce heat, cover, and cook for 4 hours. Strain, cool, and remove additional fat. Pour into 1-gallon jar, cover tightly, and refrigerate.

Meat Glaze

Cook 1 quart of brown stock at low heat until thick, reduced to 2 cups. Cool, pour into a sealable jar. Keep in refrigerator.

Roux

Mix together in saucepan:

1 cup butter

1 cup flour

Cook over low heat for 10 minutes. Cool and keep refrigerated until needed for use.

As you will notice, there are no soups included in my menus. Why? American families seem to prefer *hor d'oeuvres* to start off the meal. However, here are a few of my favorites which you may add to your menus, if you prefer.

French Onion au Gratin

Melt **3 tablespoons butter** in a saucepan and gently saute **2 large onions**, sliced.

Now add:

> **3 cups beef stock**
>
> **or 4 cups beef broth**, diluted (half broth, half water)
>
> **1/2 teaspoon Maggi seasoning**

Simmer 45 minutes. Refrigerate overnight.

Just before serving time, mix together:

> **4 tablespoons grated Parmesan cheese**
>
> **4 tablespoons grated Swiss cheese**

Heat soup and pour into 4 individual serving sized casseroles. Place on each:

> **1 slice French bread, dried in oven**
>
> **2 tablespoons of the mixed cheese**

Bake in 400° oven until cheese is melted.

Lobster Bisque

Cook **1 fresh 12-ounce lobster** in **1 cup chicken broth** for 15 minutes. Remove, saving liquid. Take lobster out of shell and dice into 1/2-inch pieces and set aside.

Cook for 3 minutes:

> **2 tablespoons flour**
>
> **2 tablespoons butter**

Add juice from the lobster, stirring well. Cook 5 minutes.

Remove to double boiler and add:

> **2 cups milk**
>
> **pinch each of salt, pepper, and monosodium glutamate**

Cook for 15 minutes. Add lobster and cook 3 minutes more. When serving, sprinkle top with **chopped chives** and a dash of **cayenne pepper**.

Minestrone Soup

In large pot, cook **1/4 pound salted pork** slowly for 5 minutes.

Then add:

> **1/2 cup each celery, diced carrots, and finely chopped cabbage**
>
> **1 medium onion, chopped**

Cook 10 minutes. Add:

> **2 quarts water**
>
> **2 cups tomato juice**
>
> **1 garlic clove, minced**
>
> **1 bay leaf**
>
> **pinch each of pepper, oregano, and monosodium glutamate**

Simmer 45 minutes. Just before serving add:

> **1 cup cooked elbow macaroni**

Serve with grated **Parmesan cheese.**

New England Clam Chowder

Boil **4 potatoes** for 10 minutes. Drain and set aside.

Melt in a pot:

> **4 tablespoons butter**

Add:

> **3 tablespoons flour**

Stir constantly, and cook for 3 minutes. Add:

> **2 bottles clam juice**

When mixture is smooth, transfer to double boiler. Add:

> **2 cups milk**
>
> **pinch each of salt, pepper, cayenne, and monosodium glutamate**
>
> **about 3 cups potatoes, diced**

At the last, add **1-1/2 pint canned, chopped clams** and cook 3 minutes more. When serving, sprinkle with **chopped chives.**

Presidential Peanut Butter Soup

I had the privilege of creating this soup in honor of President Jimmy Carter on November 3, 1976 in Winston-Salem, North Carolina. Among my most treasured memorabilia is an official letter of gratitude, on White House stationery, signed by the President himself. Was I most proud to receive that? But of course!

Saute together for 3 minutes:

> **2 tablespoons onion, minced**
>
> **2 tablespoons butter**

Add:

> **2 ounces dry Sherry**
>
> **Cook until most of liquid has evaporated.**

Add:

> **3 tablespoons smooth peanut butter**
>
> **2 tablespoons flour**
>
> **pinch of salt & pepper**

Keep stirring; cook an additional 3 minutes.

Combine in a double boiler pot:

> **2 cups chicken stock**
>
> **2 cups milk, hot**
>
> **Cook 20 minutes.**

Beat 2 egg yolks with 1/2 cup half & half (light cream). Add to peanut butter soup mixture. Cook 5 minutes.

Mince 2 tablespoons each peanuts and chives.

To serve, sprinkle each serving of soup with 1/2 teaspoon each minced peanuts and chives. Makes 4 servings.

How to Select Meat and Poultry

BEEF

First, you must find a conscientious, dependable butcher who will always give you USDA Top Choice quality. Beef should be light red in color (younger beef). Sometimes it is on the light purple side with age. Make sure that the fat is white and the marbling of fat on the lean part is fine and white. Unless the recipe calls for well-done pot roast or stew, the meat should be tender, especially for broiling, frying, sautéing, and roasting.

LAMB

Buy only young, spring lamb.

PORK

Pork must have a very fine grain and be very firm. The meat of young pork is almost white and most delicious. The older pork is more pink in color. As you know, pork is quite fat, so pick the leanest you can buy. Also remember that pork must be cooked slowly for a long time.

VEAL

Veal is normally aged from six to eight weeks to have a good quality. The meat is slightly on the gray side with pinkish white fat. Veal must also be cooked a long time because of cellulous tissues.

POULTRY

Chicken must always have smooth skin and soft legs. This denotes good quality and freshness. These qualifications apply to chicken and turkey of any weight. Duck must have white skin and soft flesh.

How to Select Fruits and Vegetables

Just two words to remember: *firm* and *fresh.*

Special Attention on Selecting Seafood

Fish markets must display all fish on ice. If you are buying a whole fish, the eyes must be clear and the meat firm. If precut, check for smell. If it smells strong, don't buy it. Lobster must be alive and kicking. Shrimps must be white and firm, as should scallops. As for clams, mussels, and oysters, make sure they are closed. If they are open, chances are that they are dead. Also remember, never overcook seafood.

Wine, Women, and. . .

Wines are just like beautiful women—some are sophisticated, while others are wild, or light, heavy, red, blonde, dark, white, younger, older, unpredictable, domesticated, and so on. Truly a meal without wine is like life without women. Just as a man becomes lonely without a woman, so, too, can a meal become lonely without good wine.

If the choice were given to fifty-million Frenchmen to choose between their women or their wine, there might be another French Revolution. I would join the revolution, because I need and want both of them.

How do you select wine? Today, it is very simple. It is much like selecting a mate. You look, you admire, you investigate the quality, age, family background, and so forth. Then you take it home or to a friend's home and become acquainted. If you find

you have made a pleasing choice, you have found yourself a companion for many meals ahead.

Buying wine is an adventure. It is definitely a matter of personal taste. For the past ten years that I have been living in the United States, I have found that there are excellent wines available from California and New York. For your own home consumption, you may wish to start with a good domestic wine. For special occasions, you may want to serve an imported wine.

Whatever you choose, my friends, make a definite gesture by serving at least one glass of wine to your loved one at dinner, not just because you know it is very healthful and better for digestion, but because you owe it to yourself and your dinner. Soon you may find that you would not think of serving a meal without its companion, wine.

How do you store wine? You need not be too fussy with domestic wines because they are young and being used rapidly. For immediate use, keep your red wine at room temperature, perhaps on the pantry floor. The bottom shelf of the refrigerator will do nicely for white or rose wines.

Your imported wines, however, are like temperamental women, and require special handling and care. Red wine should be kept on its side, preferably in a wine rack, at room temperature. White and rose wines should be chilled at least an hour before use. For red vintage wine, I suggest that you open the bottle an hour before serving so the oxygen it "breathes" will develop the full bouquet. When serving, fill the glass only half full so that you get the benefit of the aroma.

When I include wines in my recipes, please use the best available to you. For excellent results, use only excellent wine.

The Extras: Adding Spice to Your Life

HERBS AND SPICES

Herbs and spices are vital to your success in the kitchen. They will stay fresh longer and more richly enhance your food if you will keep them in tightly sealed containers, in a cool, dry place in your kitchen—not on or over the stove. This is a partial list of some necessities to have available on your spice shelf when preparing any of these recipes.

Basil	Bay Leaves
Cayenne Pepper	Celery Salt
Chives	Cinnamon, stick and ground
Cloves, whole and ground	Corriander
Fennel	Garlic, cloves and powder
Ginger, root and ground	Kitchen Bouquet™
Maggi Seasoning	Marjoram
Mint Leaves	Monosodium Glutamate (optional)
Mustard, dry	Nutmeg
Onion Salt	Oregano
Paprika	Parsley
Pepper, white and black	Rosemary
Sage	Salt
Savory	Sesame Seeds
Tarragon	Thyme

SEASONINGS AND CONDIMENTS

Here are additional seasonings and condiments which you will find important to have on hand.

Almond Oil	Bouillon Cubes, beef and chicken
Capers	Chutney
Dijon Mustard	Honey
Horseradish	Lemon Rind
Maple Syrup	Mustard, prepared
Olive Oil	Onion Juice
Orange Rind	Pickling Spices
Seafood Seasoning	Soy Sauce
Steak Sauce	Tabasco Sauce
Tarragon Vinegar	Worcestershire Sauce™

LIQUOR AND LIQUEURS

And for that really special touch in these recipes, be sure to have among your liquor and liqueurs an excellent brand of each of these:

Brandy	Chartreuse
Cognac	Creme de Menthe
Curacao	Grand Marnier
Pernod	Rum
Sherry	Triple Sec

WINE SELECTION

An appropriate wine selection is suggested in each menu.

Now you are well armed to keep on romancing with gourmet seductions!

My Super Diet

A chemical reaction of different ingredients which has worked for me if I needed to lose weight, follows. I have suffered no side effects as long as I only use it for three consecutive days and did not deviate from the menu. I have lost as much as eight pounds in three days.

I claim absolutely no financial benefits from this diet. And please note, that while others may experience some side effects from this diet, I experienced none. Therefore, I assume no responsibility for its use.

Personally, I am in perfect health, and my physician has told me that it is a very good diet for me to use. His only warning was to use it no more than three consecutive days at a time. Normally, I use this diet on Monday, Tuesday, and Wednesday and go back to normal eating for the next four days.

As always, consult your physician before starting any diet.

Breakfast
1 cup of coffee or tea

Monday:
1/2 half grapefruit
1 slice whole wheat toast
3 tablespoons peanut butter

Tuesday:

1 boiled egg

1 banana

1 apple

1 slice whole wheat toast

Wednesday:

1 apple

8 saltine crackers

2 ounces mild cheddar cheese

Lunch

Monday:

1/3 cup of canned tuna, packed in water

2 slices whole wheat toast

8 ounces iced tea

Tuesday:

1 cup low fat cottage cheese

8 saltine crackers

12 ounces cold water

Wednesday:

2 boiled eggs

2 slices whole wheat toast

8 ounces iced tea

Dinner

Monday:

7 ounces skinless chicken breast, broiled

1 cup beets

2/3 cup boiled pole green beans

1 apple

1/3 cup vanilla ice cream

Tuesday:

3 all beef wieners

1/2 cup boiled banana squash

1/2 cup boiled carrots

2 spears of boiled broccoli

1 banana

1 cup ice milk (vanilla)

Wednesday:

1 cup salmon

1 cup beets

2 spears of broccoli

1/2 honey dew melon

1 cup ice milk

10 glasses of cold water every day, and nothing else except the contents of my daily diet. Nothing else.

Best wishes,

Jacques

Aromantic Seasonings of Seduction

$\mathcal{T}$he world's food basket would be very unappealing without spices and seasonings. Imagine a French gourmet dinner without wine. I cannot!

Spices from around the world have been dominant in world trade markets since early civilization.

International chefs have been very innovative with their combinations of herbs and spices in their gastronomic creations. I, too, am always searching for unusual flavorings.

My latest creation of aromantic seasonings comes from spices exclusive to south Africa. Used for thousands of years in Africa, my spice compositions are available now in the U.S. for the first time.

My new seasonings were not created in time to include in this collection of gourmet seduction recipes. However, I experimented with the recipes in *Z'Art of Gourmet Seduction* as it went to press, and do you know what? I discovered that adding my Aromantic Seasonings to my culinary creations here, enhances the flavors dramatically. It makes other seasonings come to life. Their unique aroma and taste really bring romance to my creations, as they will to yours!

The red bottle is more potent in flavor; the green bottle is more mellow. Because the green bottle contains salt, simply reduce the amount of salt called for in any recipe to which you add it.

Use these Aromantic Seasonings, to taste, when cooking roasts, or broiling meats, poultry, seafood or fish. They can be added to soups, sauces, salads, marinades, even breading ingredients. They can be used individually, or together. I also recommend sprinkling a little on your creation just before serving.

131

You will be amazed at the dramatic results, and you will be pleased with the comments from your guests!

I believe there is no seasoning to compare with my Aromantic Seasonings of Seduction anywhere in today's market. My seasonings will enhance any type of food. Let the secret flavors in both seasonings be your secret to romance!

Bon Appetit,
Jacques

A Special Recommendation from Jacques

One final thought, my friends. If you have enjoyed sampling the gourmet recipes in this book, then you will surely enjoy the Epcot International Food & Wine Festival, held every fall, at Disney's Epcot Center in Florida. This year it will run from October 24 through November 22, 1998.

As an experienced French Canadian chef, I had the honor of representing the cuisine of my native country in Epcot's Canadian Pavillion in October 1997.

I served thousands of *Tourtieres* (savory meat pies) and other French Canadian specialties, during those 30 days of cooking and baking demonstrations. And I met thousands of people from around the world. It was a delightful experience for me. The best part of it all, though, was walking from one pavillion to the next, sampling all the delicious international foods and wines!

I sincerely believe everyone should experience this unique culinary event. Look for me there! However, I will not be cooking at the Festival this year. I am going to be sampling all the marvelous cuisine from around the world! *Bon Appetit*!

ROMANCING HEART

Shopping List

1 rose

4 large white mushrooms
1 head iceberg lettuce
1 large red bell pepper
2 large pears
1 bunch fresh parsley

2 7-ounce beef filets, center cut

1 package rice

1/4 pound (block) Swiss cheese
1/4 pound (block) Parmesan cheese
    (or pre-grated, packaged Parmesan)
1/2 pint whipping cream

1 can large, whole, pitted black olives
1 can hearts of palm
1 small jar capers
4 ounces sliced almonds

granulated sugar, powdered sugar
salt, white pepper, black pepper
butter, Dijon mustard

brandy, Amaretto
white Bordeaux wine
red Beaujolais wine

FEELINGS

Shopping List

1 rose

1 head of lettuce
   (iceberg, Romaine, green leaf, etc.)
2 medium sized fresh carrots (or 1 pound bag)
1 firm zucchini (green) squash
2 scallions
6 fresh, white mushrooms
6 large fresh, strawberries
1 fresh lemon, 1 bunch fresh parsley

12 small fresh oysters, in shell
8 jumbo shrimps, fresh
12 to 16 ounces thin-sliced bacon

1/4 pound Feta cheese
1/4 pound (block) Swiss cheese
1/4 pound (block) Parmesan cheese
   (or pre-grated, packaged Parmesan)

1 16-ounce jar marinated grape leaves
1 can large, whole, pitted black olives
1 8-ounce can artichoke hearts, plain
8 ounces semi-sweet chocolate

Greek seasoning, pickling spices,
seafood seasoning, coriander or nutmeg
Tabasco sauce, distilled white vinegar, olive oil,
butter, milk

salt, white pepper, granulated sugar, flour

MISSING LINK

Shopping List

1 rose

2 medium tomatoes
2 medium baking potatoes
1 head butter lettuce
1 small cucumber
1 bunch fresh celery
6 radishes (or 1 small package)
2 fresh lemons
1 fresh lime, 1 bunch fresh parsley

1 pound Alaskan king crab legs
2 8-ounce salmon fillets

1/4 pound Romano cheese or 1/4 cup
    pre-grated Romano cheese
1/2 pint whipping cream
1 dozen eggs

4 ounces fish bouillon
peanut oil, butter, Tabasco sauce

2 individual-size sponge cakes
    (like ones used for straberry shortcake)

brandy, Triple Sec, chablis wine

salt, black pepper, white pepper,
granulated sugar, powdered sugar,
dry mustard, paprika, bread crumbs

AN EXPRESSION OF LOVE

Shopping List

1 rose

1 head Romaine lettuce
1 bunch fresh parsley
8 ounces fresh white mushrooms
2 medium shallots
1 fresh orange, 1 fresh lemon
2 golden apples
8 ounces fresh blackberries

1/4 pound fresh scallops
1/4 pound fresh bay shrimp
1/4 pound fresh crabmeat
1 4-pound young duckling

1 package wild rice (at least 4 ounces)

1/4 pound Swiss cheese (block)
4 ounces fresh whipping cream, 2 eggs

20 ounces chicken bouillon (total)
8 ounces clam juice
1 can artichoke bottoms

white wine, blackberry brandy

seafood seasonings, rosemary, flour, sugar,
salt, pepper, paprika, butter, olive oil,
tarragon vinegar, raw honey

LONELY AT HEART

Shopping List

2 dozen roses

4 whole fresh zucchini (green) squash
1 bunch celery, 2 scallions
3 fresh, crisp apples, 3 golden pears
1-1/2 pounds red seedless grapes
1-1/2 pounds green seedless grapes
2 quarts fresh strawberries
3 fresh lemons, 4 fresh oranges
1 fresh pineapple
1 bunch fresh parsley
fresh ginger root (to yield 3 tablespoons, minced)

1 pound cooked bay shrimps
1 12-ounce lobster tail
2-1/2 pounds flank beef
3 pounds chicken wings & small drumsticks
1/4 pound (block) Parmesan cheese
     (or pre-grated, packaged Parmesan)
1/2 pound (block) Swiss cheese
8 ounces each cream cheese, French Camembert
     or Brie, swiss cheese (block), Gouda cheese

2 loaves white bread,
1 long baguette French bread

1 8-ounce can whole, pitted black olives
1 3-ounce jar each red caviar and black caviar
1 jar Maraschino cherries
mayonnaise, prepared mustard, butter, soy sauce
raw honey, dry mustard, seafood seasoning
paprika, sesame seeds, sugar

GREAT EXPECTATIONS

Shopping List

1 rose

1 large tomato
3/4 pound fresh green beans
2 large baking potatoes
1 green bell pepper
1 red bell pepper
1 head lettuce
2 endives
1 fresh lime
1 fresh lemon
2 medium bananas
1 bunch scallions
1 bunch fresh parsley

2 8-ounce fresh red snapper fillets

2 ounces Muenster cheese (block)

2 ounces almonds
1 pint vanilla ice cream

butter, olive oil
bread crumbs, seafood seasoning, paprika
powdered sugar, salt, pepper

white wine
Pernod

SPICES AND LOVE

Shopping List

1 rose

1 head bib lettuce
1 pound fresh asparagus
1 extra large baking potato
1 fresh lemon, 2 fresh limes
1 pint fresh red raspberries (frozen can
    be substituted if fresh not in season)
1 bunch fresh parsley

4 ounces smoked salmon (lox)
2 12-ounce New York strip steaks

3 ounce package cream cheese
2 ounces Roquefort (Bleu) cheese
1/4 pound (block) Parmesan cheese
    (or pre-grated, packaged Parmesan)
1 jar capers

1/2 gallon milk
1 dozen eggs

olive oil, butter, soy sauce, steak sauce,
tarragon vinegar, Tabasco sauce

sugar, cayenne pepper, salt, black pepper,
red chili pepper, rosemary, garlic powder,
bay leaves, tarragon leaves, dry mustard

red wine
brandy

DIVORCE BY CANDLELIGHT

Shopping List

1 yellow rose
1 red rose

1 head red leaf lettuce
1 8-ounce package fresh mushrooms
1 bunch scallions
1 red bell pepper
1 fresh lemon
1 fresh coconut
2 kiwi fruit

1/2 pound large scallops
3/4 pound large shrimps

8 ounces clam juice
1 can red beets, in natural juice

1 pint whipping cream
1/2 dozen eggs

1 pint orange sorbet

1 package of rice

butter, olive oil, sesame or coconut oil
seafood seasoning, paprika, dry mustard,
cayenne pepper, salt, flour, powdered sugar

rum
sweet sherry
1 bottle brandy
1 bottle orange liqueur

BODY AND SOUL

Shopping List

1 rose

6 large white mushrooms
1/4 pound fresh asparagus
1 large carrot
3 ounces fresh green beans
1 small red bell pepper
1 head butter lettuce
1 fresh lime
2 fresh lemons

6 fresh oysters, in shells
2 12-ounce, thick, veal chops
2 ounces fresh crabmeat

3 ounces Feta cheese
1/4 pound (block) Swiss cheese
1/2 pint whipping cream

1 can ripe olives
1 jar Maraschino cherries

1 pint almond ice cream

butter, olive oil, wine vinegar
seafood seasoning, Tarragon leaves, bread crumbs,
paprika, salt, black pepper, sugar

port wine
Amaretto liqueur

L'ELECTROMAGNETIC FIELD OF LOVE

Shopping List

6 pink roses, 6 red roses

1 head iceberg lettuce
shallots (for 1 tablespoon, minced)
8 ounces fresh white mushrooms (to yield 1 cup)
1 pint cherry tomatoes, 1 bunch fresh parsley
1 fresh lime,
4 to 6 fresh lemons (to yield 2 ounces juice)
1 pint fresh ripe strawberries, 2 star fruits
1 bunch fresh parsley

4 ounces Alaskan crabmeat
3 ounces cooked bay shrimp
4 ounces cooked Florida lobster meat
    (or 1-3/4 lb. Florida lobster)
10 ounces young, milk-fed veal scallop
    (ask butcher)

8 ounces clam juice
1 ounce red ham meat glaze
1 can small pitted black olives
1 jar small stuffed green olives

1/2 pint fresh whipping cream
2 ounces French Brie cheese
1/4 pound Parmesan cheese
    (or pre-grated, packaged Parmesan)
1/2 dozen eggs
1 package of wild rice
1 pint lime sorbet
butter, almond oil, beef boullion
seafood seasoning, paprika, dry mustard, salt,
pepper, flour, granulated sugar, powdered sugar
brandy, melon liqueur

143